DEFENSING THE RUN AND SHOOT

Bob Kenig

Harding Press
Haworth, New Jersey 07641

Library of Congress Cataloging-in-Publication Data

Kenig, Bob
    Defensing the run and shoot/ Bob Kenig.
        p.   cm.
    ISBN 0-9624779-5-8
    1. Football--Defense.   2. Football--Coaching.   I. Title.
GV951.18.K457   1994
796.332'2--dc20   93-44892
                                                                      CIP

ISBN 0-9624779-5-8

Printed in the United States of America

HARDING PRESS
P.O. Box 141
Haworth, NJ 07641
Books by and for the coaching profession

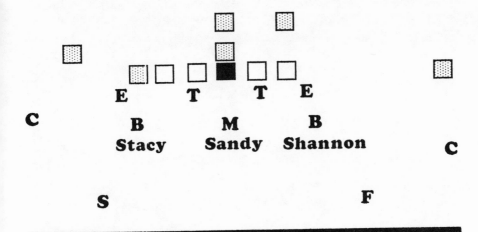

C E B T M T E B C
Stacy Sandy Shannon

S F

This book is dedicated to
Sandy (my wife), Stacy
and Shannon (our two
daughters) who are the
Backers, Tri-Captains,
Leaders and HEART of
my most important
Team, OUR FAMILY.

How This Book Will Help You

The Run-and-Shoot offense, originally conceived by Glenn "Tiger" Ellison and updated by such coaches as Darrel "Mouse" Davis and June Jones, has become THE OFFENSE OF THE NINETIES.

The Delaware Wing-T, the Wishbone, the Houston Veer, and many other high-powered offenses were created and employed on the scholastic and collegiate levels. However, unlike these offenses, the Run and Shoot has made its way to the professional leagues. The Houston Oilers and the Detroit Lions have adopted the offense, while most other NFL teams have added some phase of the Run and Shoot to their offensive schemes. In its initial season of competition, the WLAF seemed to be a Run-and-Shoot league, with many teams employing this offense. The Spring league helped boost the popularity of the Run-and-Shoot offense.

In the 1980s, Bill Manlove installed the Run-and-Shoot offense at Widener University with the help of Al Black (author of *Coaching Run-and-Shoot Football*, Harding Press, 1991). The offense produced immediate success. Being a friend and admirer of both coaches, I spent a great deal of time with them, learning as much as I could about this innovative approach to offensive football.

As a result of what I had learned, we installed the Run and Shoot at Marple Newtown High School (Delaware County, Pennsylvania), and we employed it for the two seasons prior to my becoming an assistant coach at Widener University. In both of those seasons we led our league (the Central League) and the county in total offense. Three receivers from those two years went on to play college football. Joe Sweeley, the fastest of the threesome, attended Widener, where he set numerous receiving records and signed as a free agent with the Philadelphia Eagles of the NFL.

As the secondary coach at Widener, it was my responsibility to develop defensive schemes not only to stop our opponents who employed the Run and Shoot, but also to stop our own offense. Whenever Bill Manlove and I would sit down and discuss these schemes, the person with the chalk last would win. I made sure the head coach always had the chalk last. Many of our intrasquad scrimmages and seven-on-sevens ended in a stalemate. However, we were much more successful defending against our Run-and-Shoot opponents.

The defenses presented in this book are parts of a greater defensive package. Very minor adjustments are employed to handle the Run-and-Shoot offense. Like all worthwhile defensive schemes, these can successfully be implemented against any offense. It would be impractical to develop an entire defensive package for every new offense encountered. It is much more logical to have a flexible defensive system that allows minor adjustments to cope with any offense.

Versus the Run and Shoot, we employ both an odd and an even front. We make use of multiple secondaries with man-to-man, zone, and combination coverages. We also use an extensive blitz package.

This book contains all facets of defending against the Run-and-Shoot offense. The strengths and weaknesses of the offense are totally examined. The 3–4 (odd) and Over (even) fronts are entirely explained. The one- , two- , and three-deep zone, man-to-man, and combination coverages are fully covered. Our blitz and goal-line schemes are also included. Finally, an entire chapter is devoted to our defensive disguises, perhaps the most important aspect of our defensive package.

This book is for the coach who wants to stop or, at least, slow down the most dynamic offense in use today. After reading and digesting the information in this text, if you have any questions or suggestions, please give me a call (215-353-3735). I really enjoy talking football and am always looking for new ways to stop the Run and Shoot.

Contents

Chapter 1

Understanding the Strengths and Weaknesses of the Run and Shoot

In order to stop any offense, it is imperative for the defensive coach to totally understand the basics of that offense. It is also crucial for the coach to study films (tapes) and scouting reports of the upcoming opponent to determine if the opposing coach has made any adjustments to the basic offense. This is especially true when the opposing coach employs the Run and Shoot.

For simplicity, this book refers to the two basic Run-and-Shoot sets. The Double-Slot set (Diagram 1–1) and the Trips set (Diagram 1–2) are described and motion from one of these sets to the other is also discussed. (Diagrams 1–3 and 1–4)

STRENGTHS

Vertical Stretch of the Defense

The splits of the two widest receivers (split ends) cause the defense to cover nearly the entire width of the football field. The basic rule for the split end is to split 17 to 18 yards from the ball, but never align closer than five yards to the sideline. (Diagram 1–5) The offensive coach feels this wide split alignment puts great pressure on the defense. It forces a defender, utilizing a zone coverage, to be responsible for a very large area of the field. For the defender employing man-to-man coverage, he is isolated and cannot expect much assistance from his defensive cohorts.

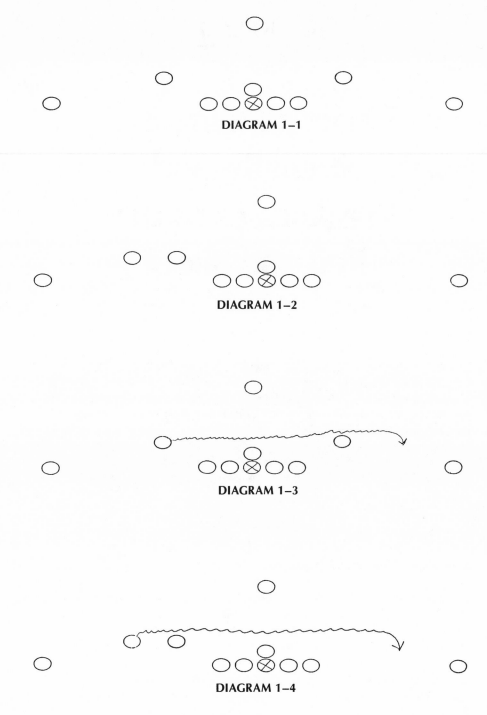

DIAGRAM 1–1

DIAGRAM 1–2

DIAGRAM 1–3

DIAGRAM 1–4

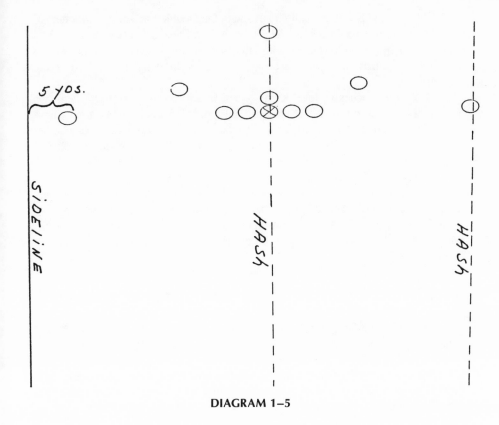

DIAGRAM 1–5

It is the job of the defensive coach to decrease the effects of the vertical stretch by reducing the area a zone defender is expected to cover and by securing help for the man-to-man defender. This task must be accomplished while giving as few cues as possible to the offensive coach and quarterback as to how it is being done. One way to achieve this goal is to disguise the pass coverages being employed. This subject is covered in detail in Chapter 9.

Ease of Changing Strength

The Double-Slot formation is a balanced offensive set with equal strength to either side of the ball. This can easily be changed, however, by putting one slot in motion to the two-receiver side of the formation and creating a Trips set and a strong side. (Diagram 1–3) The reverse is also true. A Trips set can easily be changed to a balanced set by putting one of the slots in motion to the single-receiver side of the formation. (Diagram 1–4)

The Run and Shoot normally begins with the Double-Slot set. Practitioners of the offense feel this set forces the defense to be totally balanced (five and one-half defenders on either side of the ball) and to cover the entire field. Once the offense reads and recognizes the defenses used against this set, motion is employed to create the Trips set.

Offensive coaches believe defensive reaction to the motion gives them two important pieces of information. They can determine what adjustments the defense makes to compensate for the Trips set. They also hope the motion reveals whether the defense is making use of zone, man-to-man, or a combination secondary coverage.

The task of the defensive coach is twofold. First, adjustments to the various formations must be done in a way to prevent the offense from discovering any defensive weaknesses. Second, and most important, the coach must do everything possible to prevent the offense from recognizing the kind of secondary coverage being employed. This task can be accomplished by disguising coverages and using various coverages.

Four Receivers On or Near the Line of Scrimmage

In all Run-and-Shoot formations (Diagrams 1–1, 1–2, 1–3, and 1–4), there are four receivers on or near the line of scrimmage who, by their alignment, are capable of catching a pass at any time. When any of these receivers, particularly the slots, are left uncovered (either no defender is aligned on them or a defender is aligned 7 to 10 yards off them), the quarterback may audible and attempt a quick pass to the uncovered receiver. The offensive coach believes this forces defenders to cover the four receivers tighter than normal.

The defensive coach has to come up with a strategy to prevent the quick pass while not putting the defenders in a position detrimental to stopping the entire offensive scheme. By constantly varying the distance between the defender and the receiver and by disguising the coverage, the quarterback could become confused and choose not to use the audible. Another solution is to "Bait" the quarterback to use the audible and then come up and "Crush" the receiver as he catches the ball. The receiver has his head turned to the quarterback as he catches the ball and does not see the determined defender flying toward him. A few good hits by the defender may force the receiver to be separated from the ball while seeing some "Stars." He may return to the huddle and beg the quarterback to forget the audible.

Personnel Requirements

The collegiate coach has a great advantage over the scholastic coach as far as personnel selection is concerned. The college coach recruits players who fit into his system of football. Very few high school coaches have this luxury and so must have a system into which they can plug the type of young men who inhabit high school halls.

Perhaps the two most difficult positions to fill adequately in a high school offense are the tight end and the running back. How many high school tight-end candidates are big and strong enough to successfully down-block on a defensive tackle and quick enough to run effective pass patterns while being athletic enough to hook an outside linebacker and catch passes? Many high school players want to be running backs, but do they have the qualities to be solid halfbacks or tailbacks? Are they fast enough to outrun defenders while possessing the durability and toughness to carry the ball many times during the game? Many high school programs do not have the athletes to fill these two positions, but they normally do have a multitude of little quick kids who really enjoy the game and want to play. They especially want to play where they are not going to have to block or get run over by those very large defensive linemen and big tough inside linebackers. What could be more appealing than playing wide receiver in a Run-and-Shoot offense?

On all levels of football, all players enjoy catching passes. Everyone wants to be a pass catcher. When a coach gives his players some free time before or after practice, they all run around throwing and catching the ball. This is why Quarterback–Receiver Camps and Touch Football Leagues are so popular during the summer. On the first day of fall practice, more players come out for the wide receiver positions than for any other. The offensive coach has the opportunity to select the fastest and best pass catchers as his wide receivers. However, these little "Burners" are often not the toughest players on the squad and would rather avoid contact than initiate it. This is the weakness the defensive coach must exploit.

The pass defenders must be coached to be as physical as legally possible. When a receiver is fortunate enough to catch a pass, he must pay a high price for his reception. The job of the defensive coach is to force these receivers to "Hear Footsteps" and to look for the defender rather than for the ball. When this goal is accomplished, stopping the Run and Shoot becomes a much simpler task.

WEAKNESSES

Limited Running Game

The Double-Slot and Trips formations, with true wide receiver-type personnel at the slot positions, are not designed to be power running formations. With only one running back and no tight end or tight end-like slots, the possibility of having a strong off-tackle running game is remote. The basic running game is dependent on a strong defensive pass rush. The Draw, Trap, Shovel Pass, and Screen take advantage of a strong pass rush and are often employed to slow the pass rush and make the passing game more effective. However, the running game cannot be overlooked. One look at the Detroit Lions, with Barry Sanders at running back, reveals how effective the Run-and-Shoot running attack can be.

One very effective addition to the Run-and-Shoot running attack is the Option game. Both the Belly Option, employing slot motion (Diagram 1–6), and the Slide Option (Diagram 1–7) are being utilized by some Run-and-Shoot teams. The use of the Option adds another dimension to the offense and many additional problems for the defensive team.

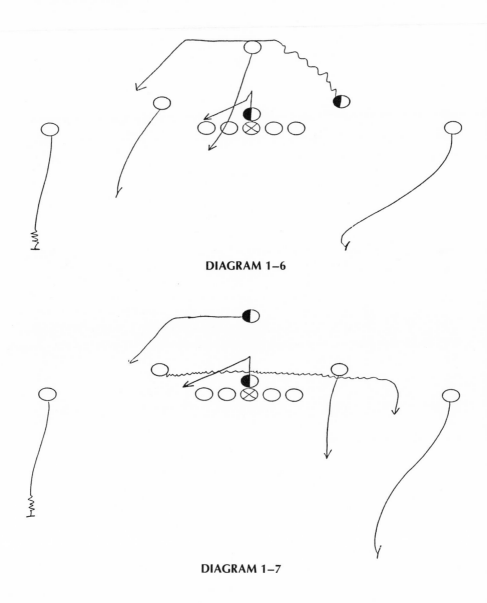

DIAGRAM 1–6

DIAGRAM 1–7

The defensive coach can never discount the importance of the Run-and-Shoot running attack, particularly when the offense utilizes some aspect of the Option game. The threat of an effective running game prohibits the constant use of Nickel and Dime packages, unless the extra defensive backs can be equally effective versus the run and pass.

The Need to Read and Recognize Secondaries

The most difficult aspect of executing an efficient Run-and-Shoot offense is reading, recognizing, and reacting to the various secondary coverages. The quarterback and receivers must perform these three activities in complete harmony, or the passing game seriously suffers. This may be the hardest part of installing the Run and Shoot or, at least, the most time consuming. This facet of the offense requires a great deal of thinking as well as split-second decisions. The thinking process may slow those speedy receivers and help the defenders. The job of the defensive coach is to slow the reading, recognizing, and reacting process as much as possible.

The defensive coach has to use every tactic available to confuse the quarterback and receivers. Disguising the coverages is the key. This maneuver totally eliminates, or confuses, all pre-snap reads by the offense and forces them to make all reads after the ball is snapped. Tactics for confusing post-snap reads are also described in this text.

Problems in Bad Weather

Since the Run and Shoot is predicated on passing, rain or extremely windy conditions can cause problems for the offense. Unless the quarterback has hands large enough to effectively control a wet ball, passing can become a problem. The receivers have an advantage on a wet and soggy field because they know where they are going and the secondary does not. However, this advantage is greatly decreased when the quarterback cannot get the ball to them. The offense could be forced to resort to its running game, which is predicated on a strong pass rush. The rush may be reduced when the defense recognizes the ineffectiveness of the passing game.

The defensive coach has to recognize when the passing game becomes ineffective and alter the pass rush and play for the run.

Chapter 2

Attacking the Run and Shoot with the 3-4 Package

THEORY

The main concern in stopping the Run and Shoot is the prevention of pass completions, particularly long ones. There are two primary ways of accomplishing this lofty goal.

The first alternative is to rush more defenders than blockers, so that there is a good chance of getting to the quarterback before the pass is thrown. Since there are normally six blockers (center, two guards, two tackles, and a running back), the defense is forced to rush at least seven defenders. This leaves only four players to defend the pass. If the rush does not get to the quarterback, a great deal of pressure is heaped upon the four pass defenders.

The second alternative is to rush very few defenders and to put those remaining in coverage. In this way the four receivers are completely covered, and the chance of getting the ball to them is limited. However, this scheme affords the quarterback a great deal of time to throw the ball and with enough time, no matter how good the coverage, a receiver can become open.

These two defensive schemes are on opposite ends of the spectrum, and circumstances may arise when either could be effective. However, if either is used to a great extent during a game, the defense could find itself in serious trouble. The best alternative is to have, as a foundation for a solid defensive game plan, a defensive scheme falling somewhere near the middle of the spectrum. This defensive scheme must have the capability of putting enough pressure on the quarterback while possessing adequate pass coverage. This scheme must also have the capacity to stop the running game. The first two alternatives, or variations of them, can and should be part of the game plan, but a more balanced scheme has to be the starting point for an efficient defensive strategy. The 3–4 Package fills the need.

THE 3–4 FRONT

The 3–4 front, with some form of zone pass coverage, is the starting point for the Run-and-Shoot Defensive Game Plan. The 3–4 front with a two-deep zone coverage is the base defensive scheme. Since this scheme employs only a three-man pass rush, it is used very sparingly during the game. A pass rush with a minimum of four defenders is much preferred. With its six-under and two-deep zone coverage, it is a good scheme to utilize in a third-down situation when the offense needs a short completion for a first down.

The variation most often employed with the 3–4 front is the firing of one of the two inside linebackers. This provides a four-man pass rush while still allowing seven defenders to cover the pass. One of the inside linebackers is designated as the "Fire-B." When a "Linebacker Fire" is utilized, the designated inside linebacker makes use of a delayed rush, and his rush lane is determined by the pass rush of the nose tackle. This stunt is not part of the Blitz Package (Chapter 7) since it involves only four rushers and is not in effect versus a running play.

Alignment and Assignment

The front seven align in a Basic 3–4 set. (Diagram 2–1) The nose tackle (N) aligns with his nose on the ball, as close as possible to the line of scrimmage. His alignment gives the offense the impression he is a two-gap defender. This is true only when he rushes the passer in the Basic 3–4 call (no Linebacker Fire).

Versus the run, the N fights across the face of the center and attempts to get to the frontside (side of the center to which the ball is run) "A" Gap. (Diagram 2–2) However, if the center gets between the N and the "A" Gap, the N jams the center into the frontside "A" Gap and keeps his backside arm free. Using this technique, the N closes the frontside "A" Gap with the center and is in a position to prevent a cutback in the backside "A" Gap. The backside inside linebacker is responsible for the "A" Gap not covered by the N. The linebacker technique is covered later in this chapter. (Diagram 2–3)

DIAGRAM 2–1

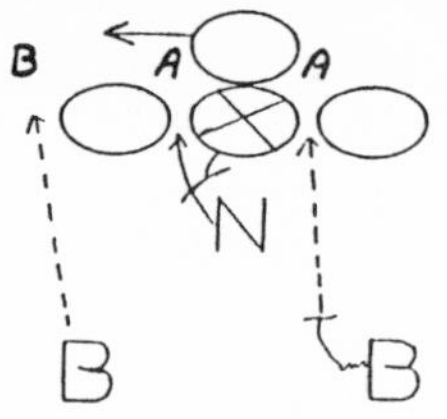

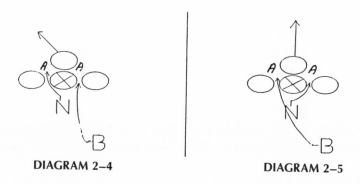

DIAGRAM 2–2 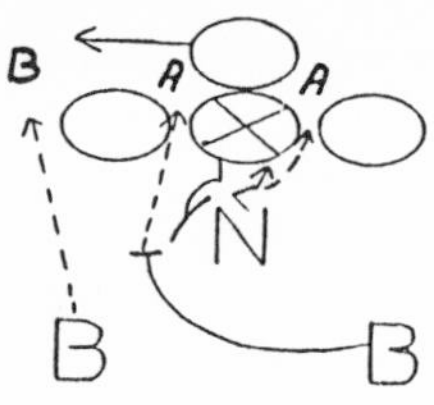   **DIAGRAM 2–3**

Against the pass, when Linebacker Fire is employed, the technique of the N is very similar to the technique used against the run. The N attempts to rush through the frontside "A" Gap on all Play-Action and Sprint-Out Passes. However, if he gets cut off, he can rush through the backside "A" Gap. On a Drop-Back Pass, he selects either "A" Gap and attacks it. The Fire-B takes the "A" Gap not taken by the N on all passes. In this manner, a four-man pass rush is achieved, with two rushers on either side of the ball. (Diagrams 2–4 and 2–5)

DIAGRAM 2–4   **DIAGRAM 2–5**

Versus a pass in the Basic 3–4 call (no Linebacker Fire), the N rushes through the middle of the center and does not disengage until the threat of Draw expires. Since this is only a three-man rush, the front is susceptible to a quarterback scrambling through either "B" Gap or in the "A" Gap not occupied by N. The inside linebackers are made aware of this possibility and must remain cognizant of it.

The end (E) aligns with his nose on the outside eye of the offensive tackle, as close as possible to the line of scrimmage. The E is responsible for the "C" Gap versus run and pass. (Diagram 2–1)

Versus run, the backside E is responsible for the backside "C" Gap but must attempt to squeeze the offensive tackle into the backside "B" Gap. Using this technique, the backside "A" Gap is protected by the N or the backside inside linebacker. The backside "B" Gap is filled by the offensive tackle, and the "C" Gap is covered by the E. Hopefully, this eliminates, or severely limits, the possibility of a cutback run. (Diagram 2–6)

When a passing play is used, the E is responsible for the outside pass rush. In all situations, he is also outside contain and can *never* lose outside leverage on the quarterback.

The inside linebacker (ILB) aligns with his nose on the outside eye of the offensive guard. His depth is determined by the down-and-distance situation, but he never aligns closer than four yards from the line of scrimmage. His key is the offensive guard on whom he is aligned and the quarterback. (Diagram 2–1)

On a running play, the frontside ILB is responsible for the frontside "B" Gap. The backside ILB is responsible for the "A" Gap not taken by the N. When the N gets to the frontside "A" Gap, the backside ILB takes the backside "A" Gap. (Diagram 2–2)

When the N cannot get to the frontside "A" Gap, the backside ILB is responsible for the frontside "A" Gap. (Diagram 2–3) This scheme forces the backside ILB to read the movement of the N. It takes a great deal of drilling during practice, but once it is mastered, it really helps prevent the cutback run through the backside "A" Gap. When Linebacker Fire is employed, it has no effect on a running play, and the N and ILB execute this Basic 3–4 technique.

On a passing play, with Linebacker Fire called, the Fire-B reads pass and then looks to the N for his key. The Fire-B goes through the "A" Gap not taken by the N. Since the ILB must recognize pass and then read the movement of the N, his stunt is delayed. This delay allows time for the Fire-B to recognize and react to Draw and Interior Screens. Also, the delayed stunt often catches the unsuspecting offensive guard off-balance and unable to pick up the Fire-B.

The outside linebacker (OLB) makes use of various alignments versus the Run and Shoot, and all are parts of the basic defensive package. Versus a slot, three different alignments are employed. The depth of the OLB is determined by the alignment of the slot. The OLB aligns as far off the line of scrimmage as the slot

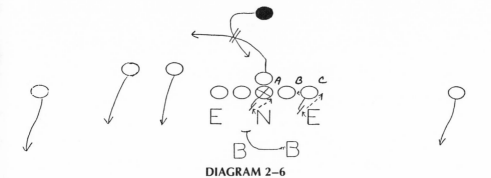

DIAGRAM 2–6

splits from the offensive tackle, but never deeper than five yards. When the slot is split three yards from the offensive tackle, the OLB aligns with his nose on the outside eye of the slot at a depth of three yards. (Diagram 2–7) When the slot splits between three and five yards, the OLB aligns with his nose on the inside eye of the slot as deep as the slot is split from the tackle. (Diagram 2–7) When the slot splits over five yards, the OLB aligns between the offensive tackle and the slot at a depth of five yards. This is referred to as a "Walkaway" alignment. (Diagram 2–8)

Two alignments are used versus a split end and no slot. Walkaway is the primary alignment, with the OLB splitting the distance between the split end and the offensive tackle, at a depth of five yards. This alignment discourages the Quick Slant and Stop Pass to the split end. The second alignment is referred to as "Ghost." The OLB aligns on the line of scrimmage as though a tight end were present. (Diagram 2–8)

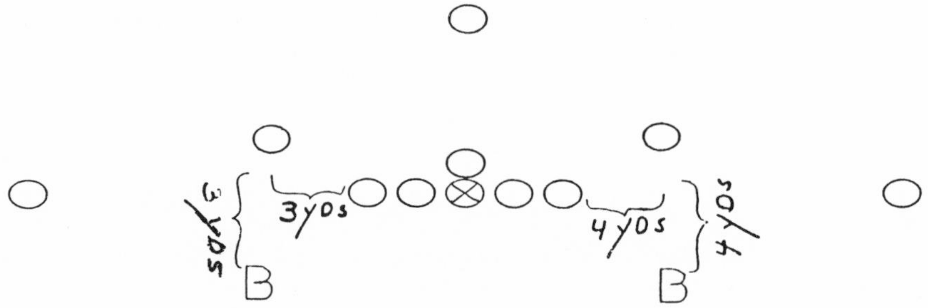

DIAGRAM 2–7

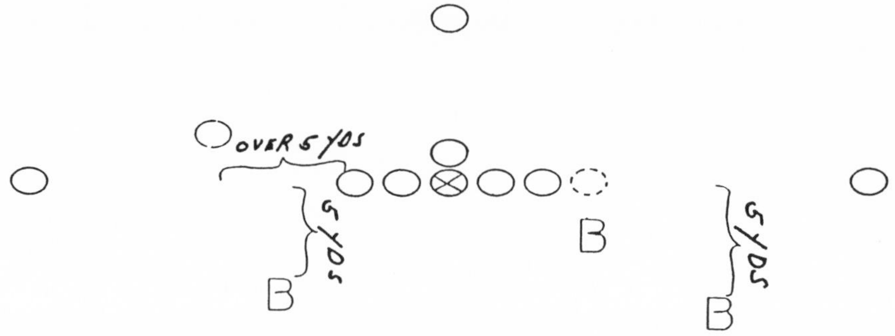

DIAGRAM 2–8

Versus a run, the OLB is responsible for outside contain ("D" Gap) and takes the first ball threat. When the ball is run away from him, he gets depth and then pursues the ball.

Situations arise during a game when the possibility of a running play becomes very remote. When these occur, it may be beneficial to replace the outside linebackers with defensive backs. These defenders may not be as effective against the run as the linebackers, but they are better pass defenders. Replacing the inside linebackers is another alternative. However, in a definite passing situation, the Draw is a strong possibility, and it is more beneficial to have strong inside linebackers in a position to stop the play.

THE TWO-DEEP ZONE SECONDARY

When the Two-Deep Zone Secondary is used with the Basic 3–4, it provides pass coverage in six short and two deep zones. (Diagram 2–9) When it is employed with the 3–4 Linebacker Fire, five short and two deep zones are covered. (Diagram 2–10) It is an excellent coverage versus the Double-Slot set, but it is not used versus the Trips set. When it is employed and the offense comes out in Trips or motions to

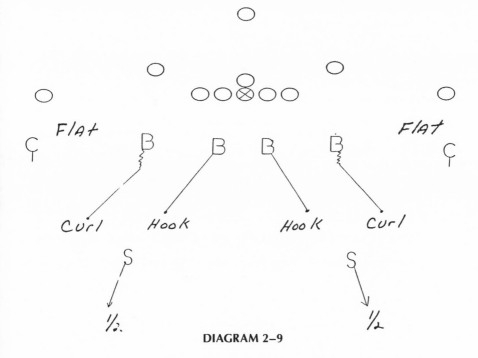

DIAGRAM 2–9

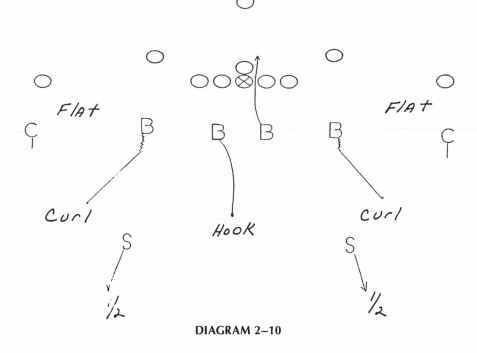

DIAGRAM 2–10

Trips, a "Check Call" (change of coverage) is made. Even though the change could be to any coverage described in this text, the normal check is to a variation of the Three-Deep Zone Secondary described in Chapter 5. For this reason, there are no explanations of adjustments versus Trips set in this chapter.

Before getting into the complete description of the Two-Deep Zone Secondary, there are certain rules all zone pass defenders must follow. They are:

1. By analyzing the offensive set prior to the snap, the zone pass defender recognizes the possible threats to his zone.

2. A zone pass defender never "Covers Grass." When there is no receiver or threat of a receiver in his zone, the defender looks to help in another zone.

3. A zone defender covers the deepest receiver in his zone.

4. When the area of responsibility is a deep zone, a zone defender *never* gets beaten deep.

5. A zone defender flies to the ball when it is thrown.

Alignment and Assignment

Versus the Run-and-Shoot offense, the job of the inside linebacker is the most difficult of any pass defender. He not only is responsible for passes thrown down the field but also has to be aware of Draws and Interior Screens.

When the Basic 3–4 is called, the inside linebacker is responsible for the Hook Area to his side. Even though the outside linebacker is aligned on the slot to discourage any Quick Pass, the inside linebacker knows how far and how fast he must go to prevent a pass completion in his Hook Zone. Once his key (offensive guard to his side) indicates pass, he checks the quarterback, slot, and finally the running back as he sprints to his area of responsibility. On a Drop-Back Pass, the inside linebackers are equidistant from the ball. (Diagram 2–11) On Sprint-Out and Play-Action Passes, the zone of the frontside ILB widens with the quarterback as the zone of the backside ILB moves closer to the original placement of the ball. (Diagram 2–12) Once the inside linebacker gets to his zone, he continues to watch the quarterback's eyes and drops as long as the quarterback holds the ball. As he drops, he looks for any receiver entering his zone and eyeballs the running back for any Interior Screen.

When Linebacker Fire is used, only one ILB remains in pass coverage. On all passing actions, he is responsible for the entire Hook Area. However, his defensive burden is lightened in two ways. The Fire-B is responsible for Draw and Interior Screens, and the outside linebackers protect the Hook Zones for a longer period of time before going to the Curl Zone. (Diagram 2–10)

The outside linebacker, prior to the snap, recognizes two immediate threats to his area of responsibility. They are the Slant Pass to the split end and the Quick Pass to the slot. The alignment of the OLB should discourage the Quick Pass to the slot.

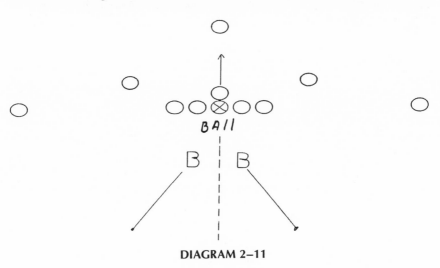

DIAGRAM 2–11

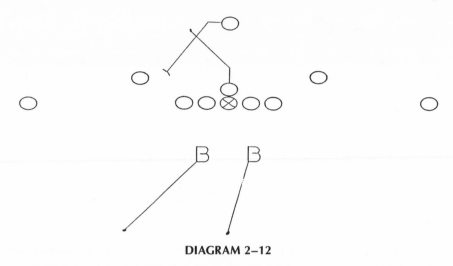

DIAGRAM 2–12

When the ball is snapped, the OLB reads through the slot to the quarterback. Upon recognition of pass, the OLB reacts to the movements of the slot. When the slot releases horizontally, the OLB flies to the Curl Zone, expecting a Curl or Short-Post Pattern by the split end. (Diagram 2–13) There is no need for the OLB to delay in the Hook Zone because the horizontal release of the slot eliminates the possibility of a Quick Pass in that area. When the slot releases vertically, the OLB drops straight back for several steps to discourage the Quick Pass to the slot and then proceeds to the Curl Zone. During his vertical drop, the OLB is aware of the possibility of a Slant Pass or Post by the split end and is ready to break on the ball. Once the OLB gets to the Curl Area, he continues to sink until the quarterback sets to throw. (Diagram 2–13)

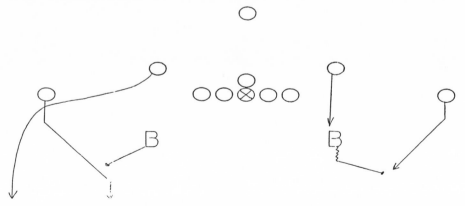

DIAGRAM 2–13

The two alignments utilized by the corner (C) are "Squat" and "Lock." When Squat is used, the C aligns one yard outside the split end and five yards deep. On the snap of the ball, he maintains his five-yard depth and waits for the receiver. The C keeps outside leverage on the split end and collides with him. When Lock is employed, the C aligns with his nose on the outside shoulder of the split end as close as possible to the line of scrimmage. The C jams the receiver as he attempts to leave the line of scrimmage.

The C reads through the split end (#1) to the slot (#2). The C makes contact with the split end and funnels him to the inside, never allowing the split end to get outside of him. The C does this while focusing on the slot.

When the slot executes a horizontal release, the C maintains contact with the split end until the C has to release him to cover the slot. This technique helps the OLB take away the threat of a Slant Pass to the split end. (Diagram 2–14)

When the slot's release is vertical, the C maintains contact with the split end and sinks with him. As he drops, the C continues to monitor the Flat Zone, looking for any delayed Screens or a Flair Pass to the running back. (Diagram 2–14) While sinking, the C wants to prevent a completion to the split end in the "Soft Area" between himself and the safety.

Against a running play, the C keeps outside leverage on the ball and attacks all plays from the outside-in. He attempts to beat any block by the split end and can never allow himself to be pinned inside. When the ball is run away from him, the C gains depth first and then pursues the ball. (Diagram 2–15)

The alignment of the safety (S) is determined by the split end, the slot, and the hash mark. The safety's rule is to align midway between the split end and slot, but never more than three yards to either side of the hash mark. (Diagram 2–16) His depth is 12 yards, but this varies according to the split end's speed and the pass patterns most commonly employed by the offense.

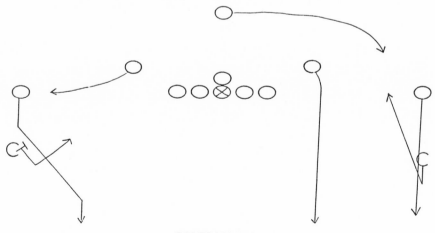

DIAGRAM 2–14

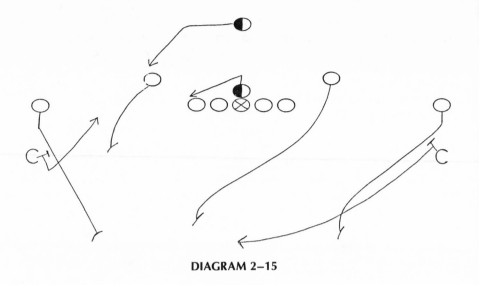

DIAGRAM 2–15

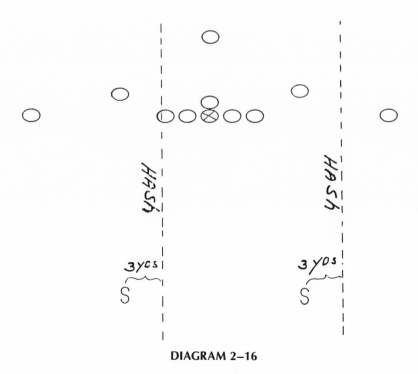

DIAGRAM 2–16

18

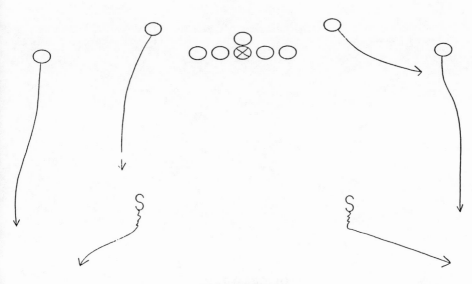

DIAGRAM 2–17

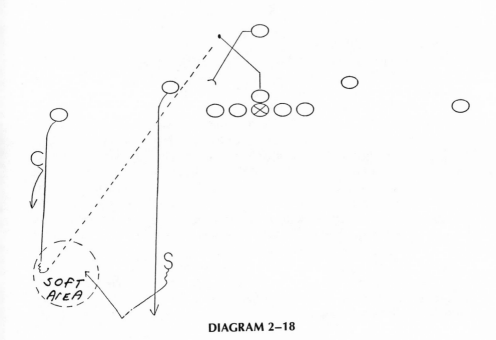

SOFT
AREA

DIAGRAM 2–18

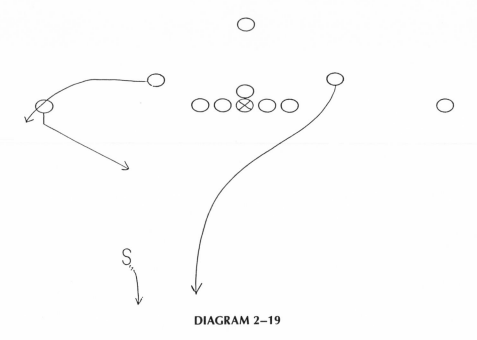

DIAGRAM 2–19

Like all pass defenders, the S recognizes threats to his Deep Half of the field before the ball is snapped. As the play begins, he reads the split end and slot to his side and the quarterback.

When a pass play begins, the S reads the patterns of the split end and slot. When both execute vertical releases, the S positions himself midway between the two receivers. He makes sure he remains deeper than the deepest receiver, and he breaks on the thrown ball. (Diagram 2–17)

A coverage problem develops for the S when the slot continues vertically and the split end stops in an area perceived to be between the corner's and the safety's areas of responsibility. Many offensive coaches attempt to attack this Soft Area when going against a Two-Deep Zone Coverage. When the C makes the proper read on the vertical release of the slot, he continues to drop with the split end but cannot totally disregard the Flat Zone. The C should end up in a position to either intercept the ball or force the quarterback to lob the pass over him, giving the S enough time to react up and have a play on the ball. (Diagram 2–18)

When either the slot or the split end executes a horizontal release, the S drops with the receiver employing the vertical release. (Diagram 2–17)

When both receivers use a horizontal release (very rare), the S looks for a Crossing Pattern by the opposite slot before he comes up to help with the short patterns to his side. (Diagram 2–19)

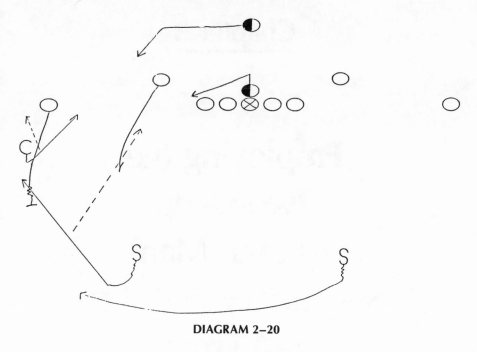

DIAGRAM 2–20

Versus the run, the S reads the movement of the C to his side. When the C goes inside, the S comes up, under control, to the outside. When the C remains outside, the S comes up to the inside. When the ball goes away from the S, he rotates through the Deep Middle Zone. He stays on the inside hip of the ballcarrier and prevents cutback. He is the last defender between the ball and the goal line. (Diagram 2–20)

Chapter 3

Employing the Two-Deep Man-to-Man Secondary with the 3-4 Front

The Two-Deep Man-to-Man Secondary is normally employed with the 3–4 Linebacker Fire front. The non-firing inside linebacker, the two outside line-backers, and both corners have the responsibility of playing a potential receiver man to man. Each safety covers the Deep Half of the field and employs the same techniques used with the Two-Deep Zone Secondary. (Diagram 3–1)

This secondary coverage is excellent in a long-yardage situation. All receivers are covered, and there are two deep zone defenders to help on long passes. When a receiver is a better or quicker athlete than the defender covering him, the deep zone defenders become an equalizer. This situation also allows the defensive coach the luxury of replacing the outside linebackers with defensive backs who should be better man-to-man defenders.

One distinct disadvantage of this coverage, used without a disguise (Chapter 9), is that it is easily recognized by the offense. By putting a slot in motion to create Trips, the movement of the defender covering the slot shows man-to-man coverage. This alerts the quarterback and the receivers to execute certain patterns. However, there are disguises discussed in Chapter 9 to eliminate or minimize this ease of recognition.

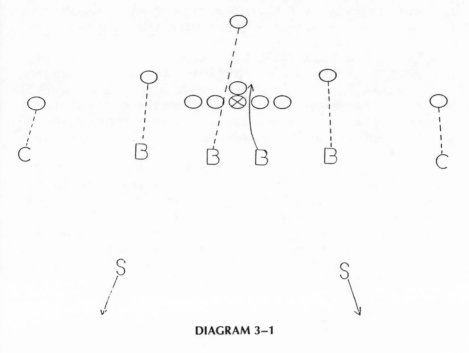

DIAGRAM 3–1

When motion is used to create Trips, the corner away from the motion is left in a difficult situation. Without any additional adjustments, he is forced to cover the split end with no defender to the inside to discourage, by alignment, the Slant or Quick Post. If this defender cannot handle the split end, a Check Call to a zone coverage or some other adjustment must be employed. Some possible adjustments are covered later in this chapter.

This secondary coverage is poor versus the Slide Option, and this is another excellent reason for not using it in a running situation when the offensive team has this option as part of its repertoire. The corners and outside linebackers are run off by the receivers and cannot leave them until the quarterback or running back (with the ball) crosses the line of scrimmage. These defenders cannot be counted on for much help until the ballcarrier is far down the field.

The responsibility for stopping the play rests with the frontside end, inside linebacker, and safety; their task is a difficult one. The E must "Slow-Play" the quarterback, buying time for the defensive pursuit. The S and ILB are responsible for the pitchman but cannot pass up the quarterback when he keeps the ball.

When a running play is executed, the frontside ILB is responsible for the frontside "B" Gap. Once the Slide Option begins, it is apparent there is no possible threat to that gap and the ILB flows to the outside. He looks to attack the first offensive player to show with the ball. He knows, prior to the snap, that when the Slide Option is attempted the frontside E has "C" Gap responsibility and will

"Slow-Play" the quarterback. The ILB realizes he must get to the pitch to prevent a long gain. The offensive team can employ several blocking schemes to greatly inhibit the inside linebacker's progress. (Diagram 3–2)

The most difficult scheme for the ILB occurs when the offensive tackle, either alone or with the guard, is given the responsibility to block him. There are a few ways the offense attempts to accomplish this goal. (Diagrams 3–3, 3–4, and 3–5) No matter what scheme is used, the ILB could be delayed and not able to get to the pitchman. This puts a great deal of pressure on the frontside safety. He must first honor the possible pass and then fly up for the pitch. This is also an extremely difficult task.

When the offense aligns in Trips or motions to Trips, the outside linebackers make the required adjustments. When the offense comes out in the Trips set, the widest slot is covered by the OLB who is normally aligned on that side. The inside slot is covered by the OLB who normally aligns on the other side. (Diagram 3–6) When the offense uses motion to get to the Trips set, the OLB who is normally aligned on the motion slot goes with him and stays one imaginary man in front of him. When the motion slot crosses the set slot, the OLB covering the motion slot "Bumps" the other OLB to cover the motion slot. (Diagram 3–7)

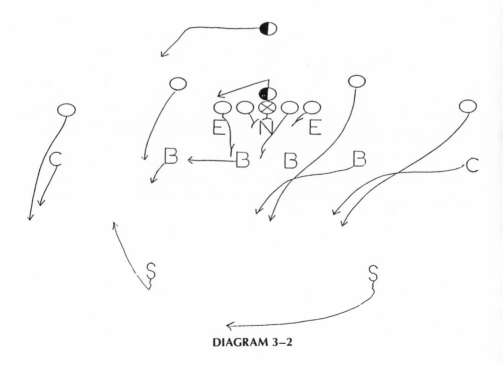

DIAGRAM 3–2

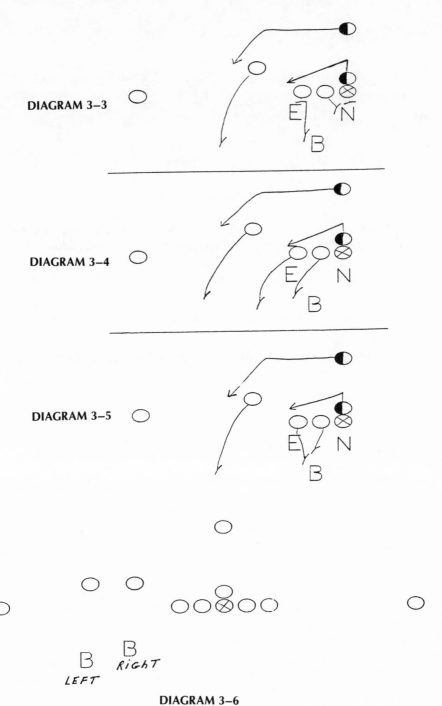

DIAGRAM 3–3

DIAGRAM 3–4

DIAGRAM 3–5

DIAGRAM 3–6

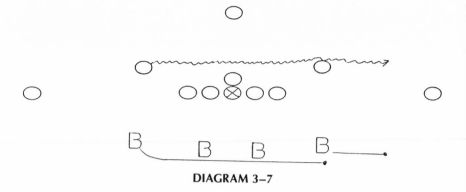

DIAGRAM 3–7

Before getting into the complete description of the Two-Deep Man-to-Man Secondary, there are certain rules all man-to-man defenders must follow. They are:

1. A man-to-man defender is extremely physical with the receiver he is covering.

2. The belt buckle of the receiver is the focal point for the eyes of the man-to-man defender.

3. If beaten deep, the man-to-man defender does not look back for the ball. He catches the receiver first.

4. A man-to-man defender flies to the ball when it is thrown.

ALIGNMENT AND ASSIGNMENT

The inside linebackers use their Basic 3–4 alignment. When the offense attempts a pass, the Fire-B executes his stunt and must check for Draws and Screens. The other ILB uses man-to-man coverage on the running back. He executes the same drop used with a zone coverage. However, as he drops he eyeballs the running back and looks for Flairs and Screens. When the running back does not release, the ILB has his normal zone responsibility.

The outside linebacker aligns with his nose on the outside eye of the slot. He reads through the slot to the quarterback for his pass or run key. His depth from the line of scrimmage varies with the alignment employed.

When Basic is used, the OLB's depth is the same as zone coverage. He aligns as far off the line of scrimmage as the slot is split from the tackle but never deeper than five yards. On the snap of the ball, the OLB backpedals and changes his position to nose on the inside eye of the slot. He maintains a two-yard cushion and continues looking inside to the quarterback until the quarterback takes more than three steps. While looking inside, the OLB simply feels the receiver rather than concentrating on his belt buckle. This technique takes away the quick passing game. Once the quarterback passes three steps, the OLB focuses on the slot's belt buckle and continues to backpedal until he is forced to turn and run with the receiver. He turns into the receiver and attempts to stay on the receiver's inside (closest to the ball) hip. The OLB does not play man-to-man defense, expecting help from the safeties. He plays as though he is in a pure man-to-man scheme. He welcomes any help from the safeties but does not expect it. (Diagram 3–8)

When Squat is employed, the OLB aligns five yards from the line of scrimmage. On the snap of the ball, he remains at five yards and adjusts his alignment in order to collide with the slot. Once the collision occurs, the OLB plays the receiver in the same manner as Basic. When he employs this technique, the OLB does not lunge at the receiver but waits to "Catch" him. This helps eliminate the possibility of missing the slot and having him run right by the OLB. (Diagram 3–9)

Lock is very similar to Squat except the OLB aligns as tight as possible to the line of scrimmage. He collides with the receiver as soon as he releases. Again, the OLB "Catches" the receiver and does not lunge at him. After the collision, he plays the same as Basic. Both Squat and Lock seriously discourage the short passing game. However, both techniques take a great deal of practice and good athletic skills. (Diagram 3–9)

When the OLB is aligned on a slot who employs motion, he runs with the slot and stays one imaginary man in front of him. The OLB makes sure he goes behind the inside linebackers and the outside linebacker. He does not want to distract them from concentrating on their keys. No matter what alignment (Basic, Squat, or Lock) is used, the OLB remains at a depth of five yards or more when he is

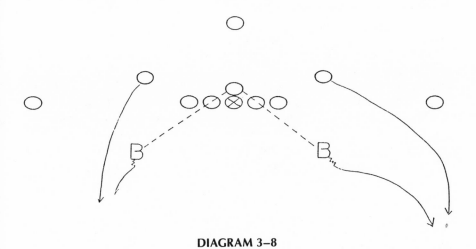

DIAGRAM 3–8

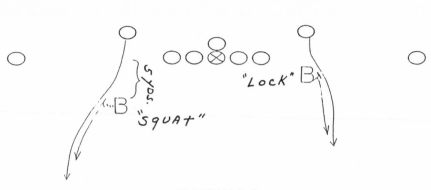

DIAGRAM 3–9

mirroring the motion slot. When the motion slot crosses the set slot, both outside linebackers employ their Basic alignment. (Diagram 3–7)

The corner uses the same two alignments employed with the Two-Deep Zone Coverage (Squat and Lock). Once the ball is snapped, the C and OLB employ the same techniques. Mentioned earlier in this chapter is the problem encountered by the C when the slot to his side goes in motion to the other side of the formation. The C is left alone with no defender aligned inside to even discourage a Slant or Quick-Post Pattern by his alignment. When the C is an excellent man-to-man defender and a better athlete than the wide receiver, no adjustment should be necessary. However, when this is not the case there are several ways to help the C with his coverage. One goal of the Run-and-Shoot coach is to isolate a good receiver on an inferior defender who is employing man-to-man coverage with no help from another defender.

One solution is called the "Loose-In" adjustment. When the slot goes in motion, the C to the single-receiver side drops to a depth of six yards and remains in man-to-man coverage. He aligns with his outside foot on the inside foot of the split end. The C is inside the receiver and in a good position to discourage any kind of quick inside pattern. He is also in a position to force the quarterback to throw any outside patterns over him. Since the C is not in outside leverage and cannot funnel the split end to the inside, the Fade or any other deep outside pattern is a real threat. To help eliminate this problem, the safety to the single-receiver side recognizes the threat and adjusts his alignment. He aligns as close as possible to the split end without breaking his hash-mark rule (Chapter 2). (Diagram 3–10)

The second solution is the "Loose-Out" adjustment. The C aligns at a depth of six yards, with his nose on the outside eye of the split end. The C remains in man-to-man coverage but is playing it with outside leverage rather than with his normal inside leverage. The safety is given responsibility for the inside patterns and inconspicuously changes his depth to 10 yards. This is one way of "Baiting" the

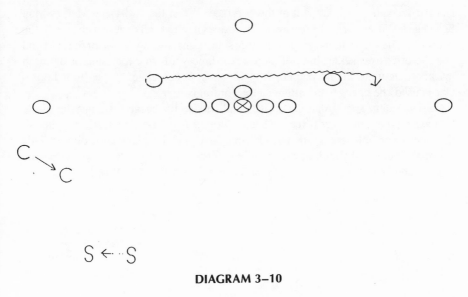

DIAGRAM 3–10

quarterback (Chapter 1) and encouraging a Slant or Quick-Post audible. When the ball is thrown, the safety flies up and "Crushes" the receiver. (Diagram 3–11)

The safety uses the same alignment and techniques employed with the Two-Deep Zone Secondary. The exception to this occurs when the offense comes out in Trips or motions to Trips. In the Two-Deep Zone Coverage, a Check Call is made

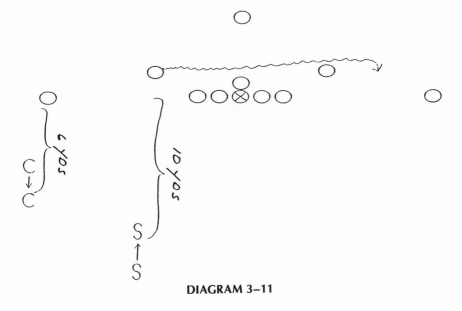

DIAGRAM 3–11

and the secondary is taken out of the coverage. When the Two-Deep Man-to-Man Secondary is used, Trips or motion to Trips does not normally cause a change in the coverage. The safety to the single-receiver side aligns midway between the split end and the offensive tackle, but not more than three yards to either side of the hash mark. He assumes his normal depth of 12 yards. When either Loose-In or Loose-Out is used, he changes his alignment accordingly.

The safety knows that the corners and outside linebackers are playing inside leverage on their receivers (except when the corner is in Loose-Out). He also knows that the vulnerable areas are outside and deep and he plays accordingly. This coverage is not as difficult as the Two-Deep Zone because the S knows he has the other secondary defenders playing man to man in his Deep Half of the field.

Chapter 4

Employing the Two-Deep Read Secondary with the 3-4 Front

Like the Two-Deep Man-to-Man Secondary, the Two-Deep Read Secondary is normally used with the 3–4 Linebacker Fire front. The Two-Deep Zone Secondary, the Two-Deep Man-to-Man Secondary, and the Two-Deep Read Secondary all look alike when the quarterback comes to the line of scrimmage in the Double-Slot set. However, there are distinct differences when the offense comes out in a Trips set or motions to a Trips set. This forces the Two-Deep Zone Secondary into a Check Call while both outside linebackers in the Two-Deep Man-to-Man Secondary align or run to (with offensive motion) the Trips side of the formation. When the Two-Deep Read Secondary is used, the only adjustments involve the linebackers and the nose tackle. These adjustments are very subtle and are made to stop the Slide Option to the side of Trips and to better handle the passing game to that side.

The combination of the 3–4 Linebacker Fire front and the Two-Deep Read Secondary is an excellent defense to use in almost any situation. However, since there are instances when there is no free safety (explained later in this chapter), it is not the best defense to use in a long-yardage situation. It provides excellent pass coverage when the offense uses either the Double-Slot or the Trips formation. It also possesses the capability of stopping the Option and all phases of the Run-and-Shoot running attack from the Double-Slot and Trips sets.

ALIGNMENT AND ASSIGNMENT

Versus a Double-Slot set, the outside linebackers employ the same alignments used with the Two-Deep Zone Secondary. Versus a pass, the OLB is responsible for the Curl Zone and the running back if he comes out to his side. The OLB has this dual responsibility because the corners and the safeties are using a form of man-to-man coverage on the split ends and slots. This allows the OLB to become an extra defender versus any of these receivers in the Curl Area. However, if the running back executes a Flair, Hook, or Wide Screen, no defender has him man to man. This forces the OLB to cover him. (Diagram 4–1) Versus a run to his side, the OLB is responsible for outside contain and takes the pitchman on any Option play. On a running play away from him, he gets depth and then pursues the ball. (Diagram 4–2)

Versus a Trips set or motion to a Trips set, the alignment and assignment of both outside linebackers change. The weakside OLB (side away from Trips) moves to a position two yards outside the offensive tackle and five yards deep. He keys the running back and quarterback and plays the run and pass in the same way he defends against them in the Double-Slot set. The strongside OLB (side of Trips) covers the inside slot man to man and uses the same alignment and techniques employed with the Two-Deep Man-to-Man Secondary. (Diagram 4–3)

Versus a Double-Slot set, the nose tackle and inside linebackers execute their normal 3–4 Linebacker Fire front and Two-Deep Zone Secondary assignments.

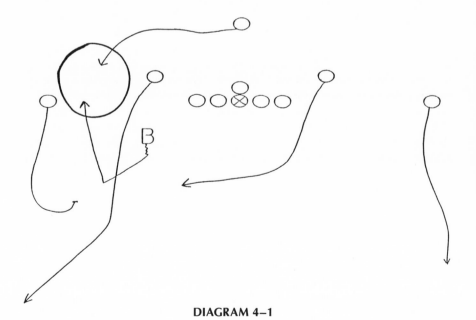

DIAGRAM 4–1

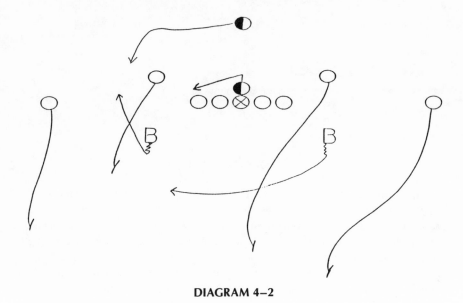

DIAGRAM 4–2

When the offense employs a pass, the Fire-B stunts through the "A" Gap not taken by the N, and the other ILB covers the Hook Zone. Against a running play, the frontside ILB has "B" Gap responsibility, and the backside ILB has responsibility for the "A" Gap not taken by the N.

Versus a Trips set or motion to a Trips set, the alignment and assignment of both inside linebackers change, but only the assignment of the nose tackle changes. The N is given the responsibility for the weakside "A" Gap on both running and passing plays. Versus a run, he attacks the weakside shoulder of the center with his strongside arm. He keeps his weakside arm and leg free and does not allow the offensive guard to Scoop or Double-Team him. Against a pass, he rushes through the weakside "A" Gap. (Diagram 4–4)

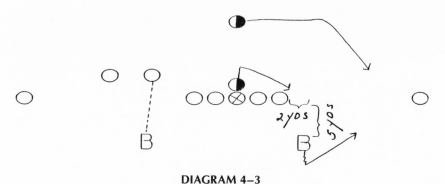

DIAGRAM 4–3

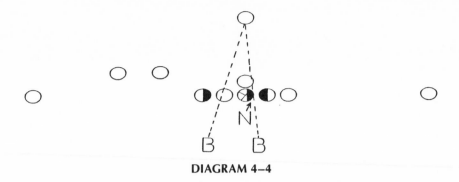

DIAGRAM 4–4

Both inside linebackers move one-half a man to the strong side of the formation. From this new alignment, they key the running back and they no longer read the movement of the N. (Diagram 4–4) The weakside ILB aligns with his nose on the inside eye of the guard. The alignment moves the ILB closer to the strength of the formation and his strongside "A" Gap responsibility, but it also reduces his chances of getting to the pitchman when Option is run to his side. However, the ILB is not needed there because the weakside OLB has outside contain responsibility and can take the pitchman. The weakside ILB is the designated Fire-B and stunts through the strongside "A" Gap on any pass. When the offense runs to his side, he is responsible for the "B" Gap. When a running play goes away from him, he has frontside (strongside) "A" Gap responsibility.

The strongside ILB aligns with his nose on the inside eye of the offensive tackle. Keying the running back and this new alignment increase the chances of the ILB getting to the pitchman on the Slide Option play. This is extremely important since the strongside outside linebacker, safety, and corner are in man-to-man coverage and their receivers take them away from the play. Unlike the Two-Deep Man-to-Man Secondary, there is no frontside free safety to help cover the pitchman. Due to the new alignment of the ILB, the offensive guard cannot cut him off and the tackle cannot step inside to block him. The offensive tackle also has a difficult time trying to go around the defensive end in an attempt to pin the ILB inside. The tackle is attacked by the defensive end and the running back steps frontside immediately, giving the ILB a very fast outside key and strongly indicating no frontside "B" Gap attack. This puts the ILB in an excellent position to successfully play the Slide Option. (Diagrams 4–5 and 4–6)

When the offense employs any running play to his side, the ILB initially has "B" Gap responsibility. When the offense employs a running play away from him, the strongside ILB covers the backside (strongside) "A" Gap.

When a pass is employed, the strongside ILB has his normal Hook Zone responsibility. Since the slots, split ends, and running back, when he releases to the weak side, are covered man to man, the ILB is an extra pass defender who actually double-covers any receiver who enters his zone. However, this changes when the running back releases to the strong side. The running back becomes #4, and the

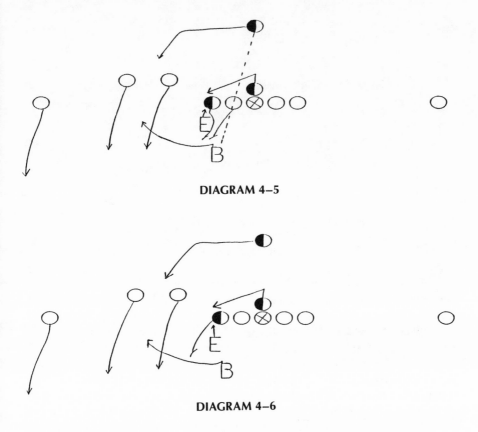

DIAGRAM 4–5

DIAGRAM 4–6

ILB must pick him up. Since there are three receivers to the strong side and the possibility of a fourth, the ILB favors this side on his drop to the Hook Area. (Diagram 4–7)

The corner uses the Squat alignment and technique and keys through the split end to #2. When he reads pass, he collides with the split end and funnels him to the inside. He separates and maintains a two-yard cushion. The C keeps his nose on the outside eye of the split end and looks inside at #2. The C reacts according to the pattern of #2. The formation determines the identity of #2.

1. In a Double-Slot set, the slot is #2.

2. In a Trips set, the outside slot is #2.

3. When motion is employed to create a Trips set, the set slot is #2 until the motion slot passes the set slot and becomes #2.

4. To the single-receiver side of a Trips set, the running back is #2.

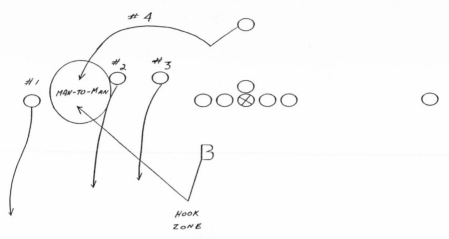

DIAGRAM 4–7

When #2 releases vertically, releases inside, or remains in to block, the C takes the split end (#1) man to man and establishes inside position on him. (Diagram 4–8)

When #2 releases horizontally, the C has him man to man. He sinks to a depth of 12 yards. At this depth, he is in a good position to help undercover the Fade pattern and give help to the safety who has the split end man to man. The C is also in position to come up to cover the short horizontal pass route and handle the Wheel Pattern when the slot (#2) turns the horizontal pattern upfield. (Diagram 4–8)

When a running play is executed toward the C, he supports as soon as the ball crosses the line of scrimmage. He attempts to beat the split end without getting

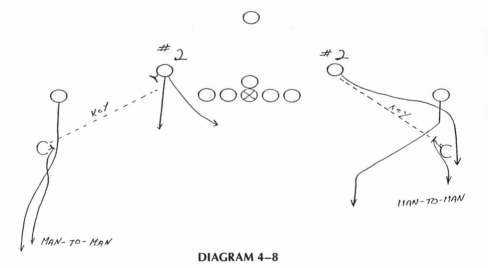

DIAGRAM 4–8

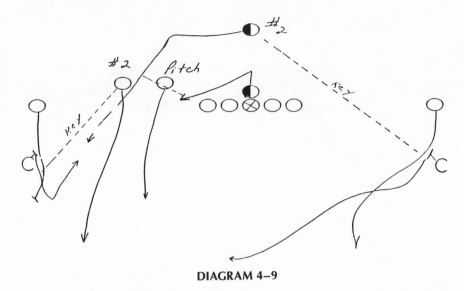

DIAGRAM 4–9

pinned inside by him. The C constricts the running lane. When a running play goes away from the C, he stays with his man until the ball crosses the line of scrimmage and then gets depth before he flows to the front side. (Diagram 4–9)

The safety employs his normal depth and aligns midway between the split end and #2 and disregards his hash-mark rule. He keys the quarterback to #2. When he reads pass, he reacts to the pattern of #2.

When #2 releases vertically or inside, the S plays him man to man. When #2 is the outside slot in a Trips set or the slot motioning to Trips (outside the set slot), the S has no inside help with the receiver. (Diagram 4–10) When #2 releases

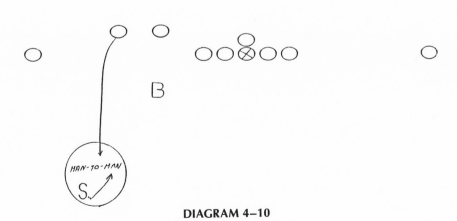

DIAGRAM 4–10

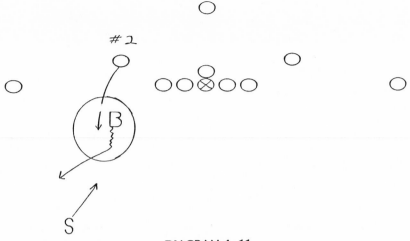

DIAGRAM 4–11

vertically in a Double-Slot set, the OLB provides help before going to the Curl Area. When #2 runs an inside pattern, the ILB provides underneath help. (Diagrams 4–11 and 4–12)

When #2 executes a horizontal release, the S covers the split end with man-to-man coverage. Since the C drops to 12 yards, he undercovers the Fade route and gives the S time to get to the split end. (Diagram 4–13)

When #2 does not release, the S becomes free and should work his way to the middle of the offensive formation. (Diagram 4–13)

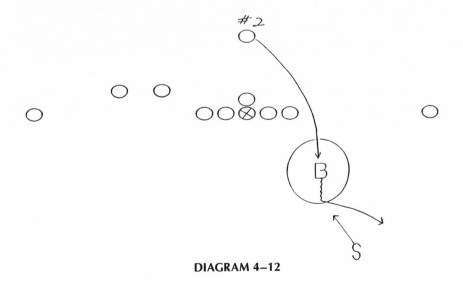

DIAGRAM 4–12

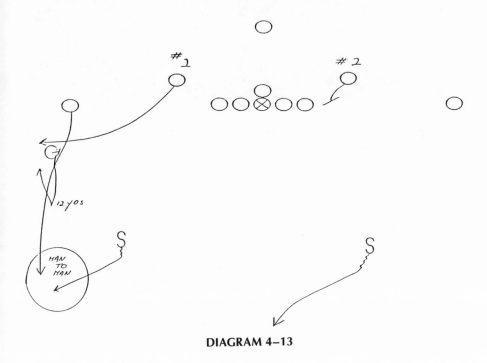

DIAGRAM 4–13

Versus a running play to his side, the S stays with his man until he crosses the line of scrimmage. The S attacks the run according to the play of the C. When the C goes inside, the S goes outside and vice versa. (Diagram 4–14) When the ball is run away from the S, he again stays with his man until the ball crosses the line of scrimmage. He rotates through the deep middle and stays on the inside hip of the ballcarrier and eliminates any cutback. (Diagram 4–14)

The key to success in employing the Read Secondary is recognition and communication between the C and the S. Both defenders are expected to make the correct reads. However, the C calls out the pattern of #2 so the S knows who to cover. The call of C is never incorrect. Whatever the C calls, the S reacts accordingly. To effectively work this process, a great deal of practice time is required. Once the process is mastered, it is well worth the effort.

Unlike the Two-Deep Zone and the Two-Deep Man-to-Man Secondaries that are employed by many teams, the Two-Deep Read Secondary is not as conventional and may require further discussion to be totally understood. For this reason, the combination of the 3–4 Linebacker Fire front and the Two-Deep Read secondary is explained versus a common Run-and-Shoot running and passing play, and each defender's assignment is analyzed.

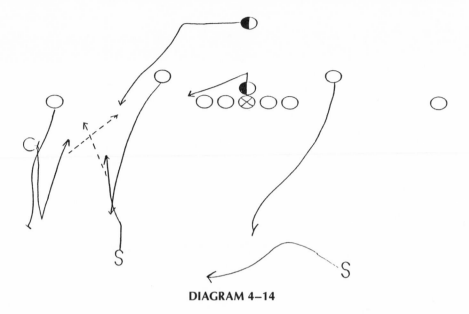

DIAGRAM 4–14

SLIDE OPTION TO THE TRIPS SIDE

The N attacks the weakside shoulder of the center and covers the backside "A" Gap. The backside E attacks the backside tackle and squeezes him into the backside "B" Gap. The frontside E executes his technique on the offensive tackle and prevents him from getting to the frontside ILB. When the frontside E recognizes Slide Option to his side, he takes a step back off the line of scrimmage and "Slow-Plays" the quarterback, buying time for the defensive pursuit. By stepping off the line of scrimmage, the E puts himself in an excellent position to play the quarterback and also to get to the running back if a premature pitch occurs.

The frontside ILB reads the movement of the running back and makes sure the frontside "B" Gap is not being attacked. He slides to the outside and is in a good position to take the running back if the ball is pitched to him. The ILB never crosses the line of scrimmage to tackle the pitchman. This limits the possibility of the running back beating the ILB to the sideline and making a big play.

The backside ILB reads the movement of the running back and flows to the frontside "A" Gap. Once he is sure that all possible threats to that gap have disappeared, he gets into the proper angle of pursuit.

The backside OLB drops as he reads a running play going away. He looks for a Reverse or any Counter play as he is dropping. When the OLB is sure the threat of these plays has passed, he properly pursues the Slide Option.

The frontside OLB, S, and both corners employ man-to-man coverage on their receivers and go to the ball once the ballcarrier crosses the line of scrimmage.

The backside S rotates through the deep middle, stays on the inside hip of the ballcarrier, and looks for a cutback. (Diagram 4–15)

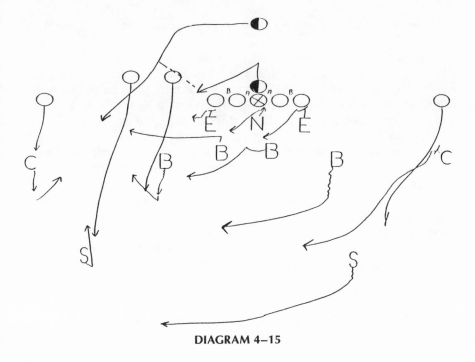

DIAGRAM 4–15

SLIDE PASS FROM A TRIPS SET

Like nearly all Run-and-Shoot patterns, the individual pass routes are determined by the secondary being employed. Since the Read Secondary gives the appearance of a zone coverage, the Slide Pass is analyzed in this chapter as though it is read as a zone. Since the Read Secondary is actually a form of man-to-man coverage, the passing play is also analyzed as though it is read as man-to-man coverage.

When the offense reads the coverage as a Two-Deep Zone, the strongside split end (#1) starts his route with a five-yard vertical release. The strongside C collides with #1 and funnels him to the inside. During this time, the strongside C is reading the release of the outside slot (#2). When the C reads the horizontal release of #2, the C calls it out to the strongside S to tell the S he must cover #1. As the strongside C disengages from #1, he drops and watches the Fish Hook Pattern of #2. The C puts himself in a position to easily come up if the ball is thrown to #2 on or near the line of scrimmage and deep enough to prevent the slot from going long and beating him.

The strongside split end (#1), after being hit by the strongside C and getting to a depth of five yards, begins to run a Post Pattern. Since #1 believes the secondary is using zone coverage, he looks for an open area—a soft spot in the zone—to stop and catch the ball. However, it is really man-to-man coverage and there is no open area. When both the quarterback and #1 read this as a zone and the ball is thrown into what is perceived to be an open area, an interception by the S is a real possibility.

The strongside outside linebacker covers the inside slot (#3) man to man. His alignment should discourage an audible Quick Pass to #2. If it does not, a disguise may be employed, or the strongside S can align at eight yards rather than at his normal depth. As #3 releases vertically, he is covered by the OLB. The ILB, dropping to the Hook Zone, should give some inside help to the OLB.

The weakside split end (#1) runs a deep outside pattern and the setback (#2) blocks to the front side. The weakside C calls the action of #2 and takes #1 man to man. Since #2 (setback) is not running a pattern to the weak side, the weakside S becomes free and may be able to give some deep assistance to the strongside OLB covering #3. The weakside OLB drops to the Curl Area. Since there is no threat to that area, he continues to sink and provides additional coverage on weakside #1. (Diagram 4–16)

When the offense reads the coverage as man to man, the strongside split end (#1) runs the same pattern employed against a zone. However, he shortens the Post portion of the route and breaks deep in an attempt to clear the short area. The strongside C funnels #1 and reads the horizontal release of #2. The C calls out the horizontal release of #2 and begins to drop as he recognizes the pattern of #2 as a Wheel and not a Fish Hook. He is in an excellent position to effectively play the outside slot.

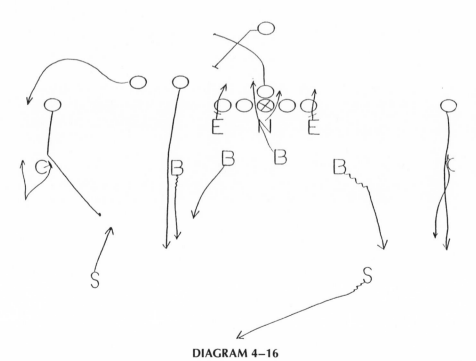

DIAGRAM 4–16

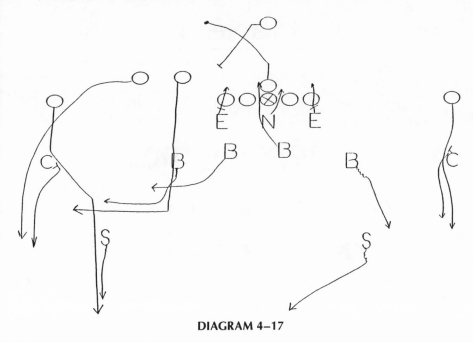

DIAGRAM 4–17

The strongside S reacts to the call of the C and the pattern of the split end. The S picks up #1 and takes him deep.

The strongside OLB has the most difficult assignment, covering the inside slot (#3). Versus the man-to-man secondary, the Run-and-Shoot quarterback wants to hit #3. The inside slot executes a hard vertical release, trying to drive the OLB deep. Between 8 and 12 yards, #3 executes a 90-degree cut away from the OLB. Since the OLB is playing on the inside of #3, the slot runs his pattern to the outside. The OLB breaks with him and ends up in a position between the slot and the quarterback. The OLB is in a position to force the quarterback to throw the ball over him. If the quarterback attempts to lob the ball, it could be intercepted by the OLB, or the C could react up to the ball and pick it off.

The ILB, not wanting to "Cover Grass," should also be in a position to force a high throw by the quarterback. The ILB is also positioned between the quarterback and #3.

The backside split end runs the same pattern versus man-to-man coverage and zone coverage. Therefore, the backside coverage is the same. (Diagram 4–17)

Chapter 5

Stopping the Run and Shoot with the Over Package

THEORY

The Over front with the Three-Deep Zone Secondary, like the 3–4 Linebacker Fire front with the Two-Deep Zone Secondary, puts sufficient pressure on the quarterback while providing adequate pass coverage. This even, eight-man front also possesses the capability of stopping the Run-and-Shoot running attack.

Unlike the 3–4 Package, which requires a stunt by the inside linebacker to get a fourth pass rusher, the Over front provides four immediate pass rushers. One of these attackers is the best pass-rushing OLB. The strong pass rush, coupled with three pass defenders in the Deep Zones, makes this an excellent defensive scheme to employ in a passing situation.

The Over Package is also formidable against the run, particularly versus a Double-Slot set. The 3–4 Package, because it is a seven-man front, forces the offside end to cover two gaps. He takes the offside "C" Gap and squeezes the offside offensive tackle into the "B" Gap. (Diagram 2–6) Versus a Double-Slot set, the Over front provides a single-gap responsibility for each front defender. (Diagram 5–1) This makes it very difficult for the offense to execute a successful inside running game.

When the ball is on the hash mark, employing the Over front allows the defensive coach the flexibility of putting the best outside linebacker and strong safety (the toughest secondary defender) to the wide side of the field. This puts the

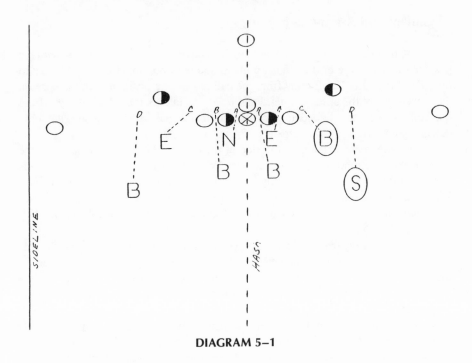

DIAGRAM 5–1

two best defenders to the area on the field most often attacked by offensive teams. When the ball is in the middle of the field and the offense has a strong right- or left-handed tendency, the Over front allows the coach to place these two defenders to the side of the defense he feels will be attacked by the offensive team. (Diagram 5–1)

When the defense employs the 3–4 front and the Two-Deep Zone Secondary and the offense makes use of Trips, the defense must make a Check Call and change the secondary coverage. This is not true with the Over front and the Three-Deep Zone Secondary. However, some adjustments are required by certain defenders, and these are totally covered in this chapter.

THE OVER FRONT

The Over front is created by shifting the 3–4 odd front to an even front. The direction of the shift is determined by the field position and the right- or left-handed tendency of the offensive team. Normally, when the ball is on the hash mark, the front shifts to the sideline. When the ball is in the middle of the field, the front normally shifts away from the side the offense has a tendency to attack. Shifting in these two ways allows the best outside linebacker and strong safety to always align to the side the offense has a tendency to attack.

Alignment and Assignment

The three defensive linemen shift to the side of the call. The N aligns with his nose on the inside eye of the offensive guard and is responsible for the "A" Gap to the side of the call. The E away from the call moves to a position with his nose on the outside eye of the offensive guard and is responsible for the "B" Gap away from the call. These two defenders provide the inside pass rush and are the only defenders not affected by a Trips set.

The alignment of the E to the side of the call is a bit more complex than the alignment of the other two down linemen. When the slot is split up to two yards from the offensive tackle, the E aligns with his nose on the inside eye of the slot. When the slot is split more than two yards, the E moves to his normal 3–4 alignment on the offensive tackle. In both alignments, he is responsible for the "C" Gap. (Diagram 5–2)

The OLB away from the call employs the same alignments as the E to the side of the call. However, there is one minor difference. The E operates from a three- or four-point stance while the OLB normally uses a two-point stance. The E and the OLB provide the outside pass rush and are responsible for the quarterback on an Option play.

When facing a Double-Slot set, the ILB aligns in the same alignment used with the 3–4 front. He aligns with his nose on the outside eye of the offensive guard. His depth is determined by the down and distance, but he never aligns closer than four yards from the line of scrimmage. In the Over front, unlike the 3–4, the offensive guards are covered by defensive linemen (N and E). This eliminates the offensive guard as an effective key for the ILB. The ILB switches his attention from the guard to the setback and uses the setback as his initial key. Versus a running play, the ILB to the side of the call is responsible for the "B" Gap. The ILB away from the call covers the "A" Gap to his side.

Against a Double-Slot set, the alignment of the OLB to the side of the call is determined by the alignment of the slot. When the slot is split up to two yards from the offensive tackle, the OLB positions himself two yards outside the slot and six yards deep. (Diagram 5–3) When the slot splits more than two yards, the OLB

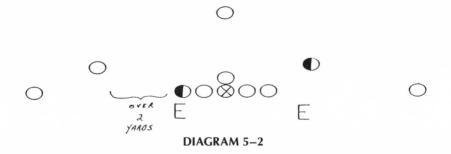

DIAGRAM 5–2

DIAGRAM 5–3

aligns with his nose on the outside eye of the slot and remains six yards deep. (Diagram 5–4) The OLB keys through the slot to the quarterback. When the ball is run to his side, the OLB attacks the play from the outside-in. When the ball is run away from him, the OLB gains depth and pursues the ball, always aware of a cutback or Counter play.

The strong safety (SS) always aligns to the side away from the call and employs the same alignments and keys as the OLB to the side of the call. Both are responsible for the "D" Gap and take the pitchman on any Option play.

Alignments vary for some members of the defensive front when they face a Trips set or motion to a Trips set. (Diagrams 5–5 and 5–6)

When facing Trips to his side, the E to the side of the call (the OLB away from the call) aligns with his nose on the outside eye of the offensive tackle (3–4 alignment). Versus Trips, the E or OLB disregards the inside slot and moves to his alignment on the offensive tackle when he hears the ILB yell "In" to him.

The alignment and assignment of both inside linebackers change versus a Trips set. When the Run-and-Shoot offense comes out in or motions to a Trips set, the ILB away from the Trips moves to position directly over the offensive center and

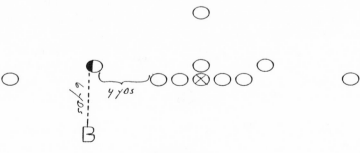

DIAGRAM 5–4

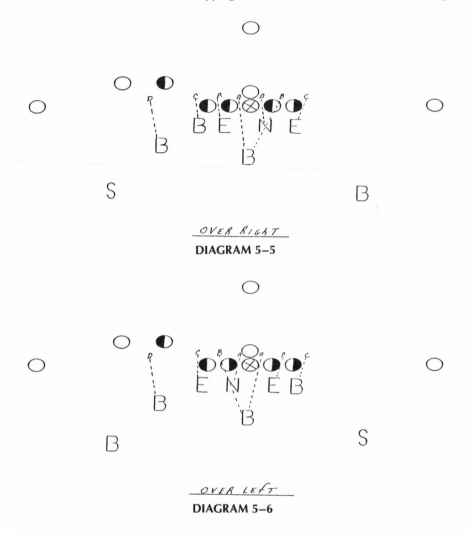

OVER RIGHT

DIAGRAM 5–5

OVER LEFT

DIAGRAM 5–6

becomes a middle linebacker (MLB) with a two-gap responsibility. The MLB assumes responsibility for two inside gaps ("B" Gap to the side of the call and "A" Gap away from the call), previously covered by two inside linebackers versus a Double-Slot set. Since the center is not covered by a defensive lineman, he becomes the key for the MLB. With his dual inside-gap responsibility, the MLB is not expected to give much assistance on an outside running play. He must make sure there is no threat to either inside gap before he pursues to the outside. (Diagram 5–7)

The ILB to the side of the Trips aligns with his nose on the outside eye of the inside slot (#3). He aligns as far off the line of scrimmage as the slot is split from the offensive tackle, but never deeper than five yards. His first responsibility is to

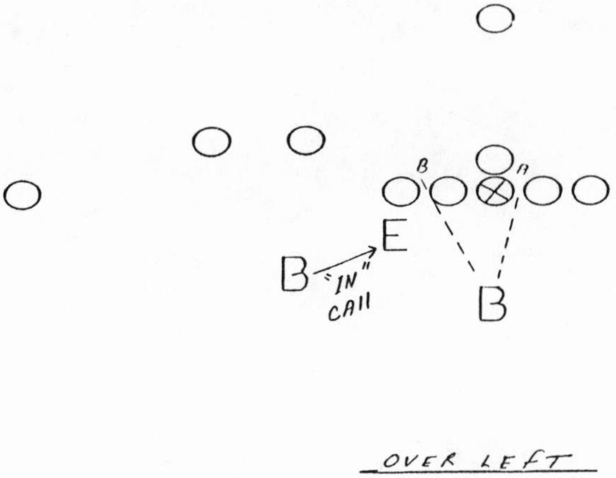
B
A
E
B
"IN"
CAll
B
OVER LEFT

DIAGRAM 5–7

call "In" to either the E or OLB who is aligned on the inside slot. The ILB keys through the slot to the quarterback and is responsible for the "D" Gap when the ball is run to his side. When the ball is run away from him, the ILB gets depth and pursues the ball.

The alignment of both the OLB to the side of the call and the SS changes when the offense employs Trips. This is true when aligned to the side of Trips or the single-receiver side. When positioned on the Trips side, the OLB or SS aligns with his nose on the outside eye of the outside slot (#2) at a depth of six yards and still keys through the slot to the quarterback. (Diagram 5–8)

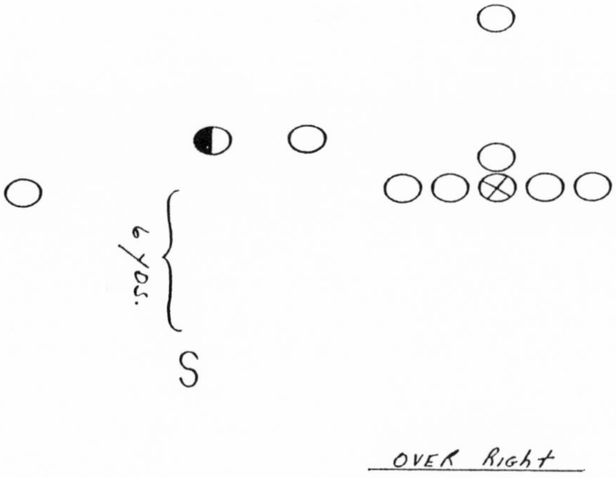
6 YDS.
S
6 YDS
B
OVER Right

DIAGRAM 5–8

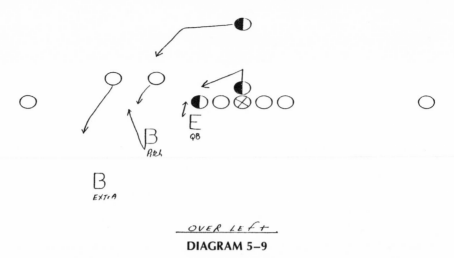

OVER LEFT

DIAGRAM 5–9

When the offense employs the Slide Option play to the side of the Trips, either the OLB (to the side of the call) or the SS is an extra defender. The ILB, who has adjusted to the outside, is expected to take the pitchman. (Diagram 5–9)

On the single-receiver side (side away from Trips), the OLB (to the side of the call) or the SS aligns midway between the offensive tackle and the split end (#1) at a depth of six yards. From this position he looks into the backfield and keys the quarterback. When Slide Option is run to his side, he is responsible for the pitchman. (Diagram 5–10)

In a definite passing situation, it is practical to replace both outside linebackers with defensive backs when using the 3–4 front. This provides better pass coverage. The same "Situational Substitution" applies when the Over front is employed. However, only the OLB to the side of the call need be replaced.

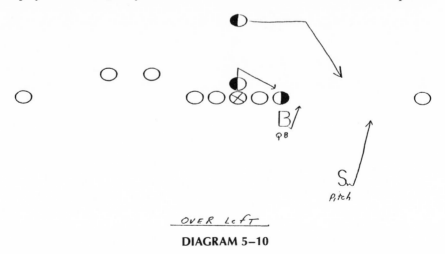

OVER LEFT

DIAGRAM 5–10

Remember, the other OLB (to the side away from the call) should be the best pass rusher and a real asset in a passing situation.

THE THREE-DEEP ZONE SECONDARY

When the Three-Deep Zone Secondary is employed with the Over front, it provides pass coverage in four short zones and three deep zones. (Diagram 5–11) When it is used and the offense comes out in Trips, the secondary remains effective. However, Trips or motion to Trips causes some modification in both alignments and assignments. For this reason, alignments and assignments are covered in this chapter versus a Double-Slot set and a Trips set.

Versus a Double-Slot Set

Alignment and Assignment

When the ILB recognizes a Drop-Back Pass, he sprints through the Hook Zone to the Curl Zone. When a receiver crosses his face in the Hook Area, the ILB covers the receiver until the receiver vacates the zone. The ILB then proceeds to the

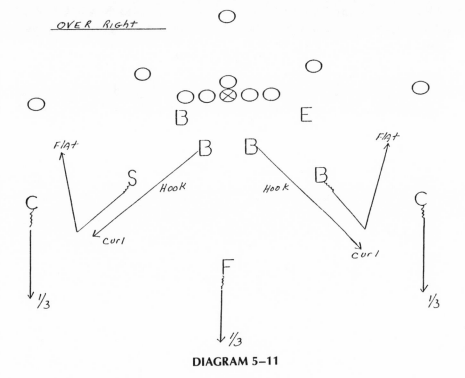

DIAGRAM 5–11

Curl Area. When there is no receiver in the Hook Zone, the ILB goes directly to the Curl Zone. During his pass drop, the ILB watches the quarterback's eyes and any potential threats to his area of responsibility. Once he reaches the Curl Zone and the ball is not yet thrown, the ILB continues to watch the quarterback and drops as long as the quarterback holds the ball. He remains mindful of any underneath patterns. (Diagram 5–12)

When the quarterback executes a Sprint-Out or Play-Action Pass, the ILB to the onside (side of the offensive play) uses the same techniques employed versus a Drop-Back Pass. The ILB to the offside (side away from the offensive play) executes a different technique. He drops into the "Hole," an area directly over the offensive center. The ILB looks to the offside slot to see if he is running a vertical or Crossing Pattern. When the ILB sees there is no vertical or Crossing Pattern, he continues to drop and is aware of both onside and offside receivers. (Diagram 5–13)

The OLB to the side of the call and the SS react in the same manner to passes. As either defender reads a Drop-Back Pass, a Sprint-Out or Play-Action Pass to his side, he reacts to the movement of the slot (#2). His reaction is very similar to the OLB in the Two-Deep Zone Secondary (Chapter 2) with one very significant exception.

When the slot releases vertically, the OLB or SS drops straight back for a few steps to discourage a Quick Pass to the slot and to occupy the Hook Area until the ILB is in position to cover the zone. The OLB or SS then proceeds to the Curl Zone. Since the slot is in the Hook Area, the ILB covers the slot until he vacates the zone. This forces the ILB to get to the Curl Zone very late or not at all. Therefore, the OLB or SS is forced to become the primary defender of the Curl Area. Unlike the Two-Deep Zone Secondary, the Three-Deep Zone Secondary forces one defender to cover two areas when the slot executes a vertical release. The OLB to the side of the call or the SS is responsible for the Curl and Flat Zones. As the defender sinks, he

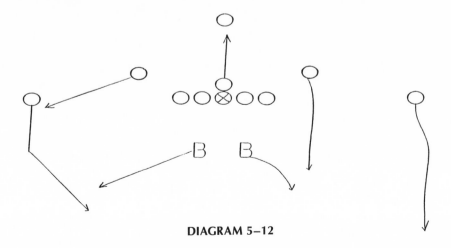

DIAGRAM 5–12

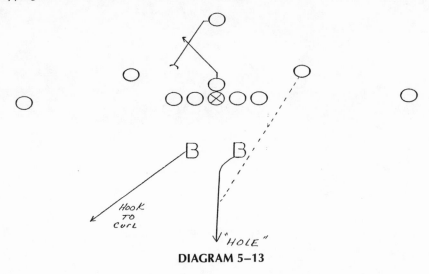

DIAGRAM 5–13

knows the Flat Area could be attacked by the setback (Screen or Flair), and the OLB or SS, along with the ILB covering the Hook Area, must react up if the ball is thrown to the Flat Zone. (Diagram 5–14)

When the slot executes a horizontal release, the OLB or SS drops immediately to the Curl Area to protect the zone prior to the arrival of the ILB. As the OLB or SS drops, he remains very aware of the slot. The defender's main area of responsibility is the Flat Zone, but a completion in the Curl Area represents a

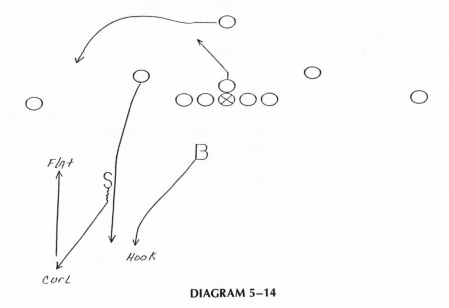

DIAGRAM 5–14

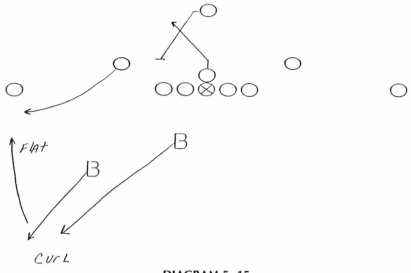

DIAGRAM 5–15

greater initial offensive gain than a completion in the Flat Area. Once the OLB or SS feels the ILB coming into the Curl Zone or sees a pass thrown into the Flat Area, he sprints to the receiver in the Flat Zone. When a receiver does make a catch in the Flat Area, the OLB or SS must make the receiver "Pay the Price" for the reception. This often discourages any short passes in the Flat Zone. (Diagram 5–15)

When the OLB to the side of the call or the SS reads a Sprint-Out or Play-Action Pass away, his areas of responsibility are still the Curl to Flat Zones, and he still keys through the slot to his side.

When the quarterback executes a Sprint-Out or Play-Action Pass and the slot releases inside (Crossing Pattern), the OLB or SS yells "Fire" to the ILB occupying the Hole. This makes the ILB aware of a receiver coming into his area of responsibility. The onside OLB or SS sprints to the Curl Area and then checks the Flat Zone before continuing to drop straight back. The offside OLB or SS employs a "Comeback Technique." This technique is used as the defender sprints to the Curl Area. The OLB or SS focuses his attention on the split end and then on the offside Flat Zone. When the split end runs an inside pattern under 15 yards or runs a Hitch Pattern under 15 yards, the defender takes him man to man. When the split end runs an outside route under 15 yards, the OLB or SS gets between the ball and the receiver, forcing the quarterback to throw the ball high. It is extremely difficult for a quarterback to sprint out in one direction and throw the ball in the opposite direction to a receiver running away from him. When the split end goes deeper than 15 yards, the defender disregards the receiver, knowing the C in the Deep Zone will cover him.

When the threat of the split end disappears, the OLB or SS turns his attention

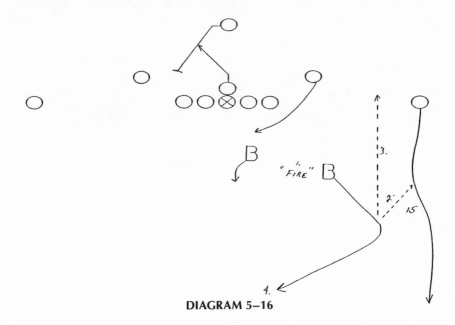

DIAGRAM 5–16

to the offside Flat Zone. When a receiver enters that zone, the OLB or SS takes him man to man. When there is no receiver in the Flat Zone, the defender turns and sprints toward the Deep Middle to help in another zone. Remember, no pass defender is ever permitted to "Cover Grass." (Diagram 5–16)

When the slot executes a vertical release, the OLB or SS calls "Fire" to the ILB occupying the Hole. Again, this alerts the ILB to look for the slot and get between him and the quarterback. The OLB or SS drops with the slot for several steps to discourage a Quick Pass and then executes his normal Comeback Technique.

When the slot releases horizontally, the OLB or SS drops immediately to the Curl Area. Remember, the ILB is in the Hole and he does not come out to cover the Curl Area. This puts additional pressure on the OLB or SS to the offside. As the defender drops, he remains aware of the Flat Zone but realizes it is more important to take the deeper (Curl Area) pass threat away first. If the ball is thrown in the Flat Zone, the OLB or SS comes up and tackles the receiver for a short gain. However, if the defender comes up and covers the slot in the Flat Area and a pass is completed in the Curl Area, a long gain is a very strong possibility. When there is no longer a threat to either the Curl or Flat Zones, the OLB or SS continues to drop and looks to help in another zone. (Diagram 5–17)

The corner (C) aligns with his nose on the outside eye of the split end (#1) at a depth of eight yards. This alignment changes for the C who aligns to the sideline side of the hash mark when the ball is located on the hash mark. The C maintains his normal alignment until the split end aligns within six yards of the sideline.

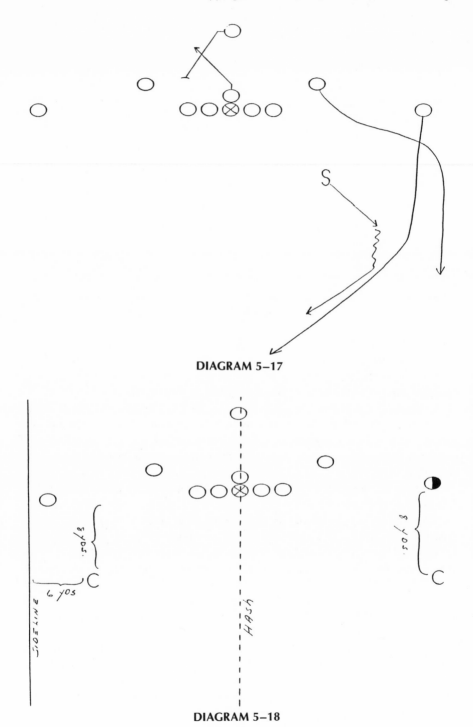

DIAGRAM 5–17

DIAGRAM 5–18

When this occurs, the C remains six yards from the sideline and allows the sideline to act as another defender. This is called the "Sideline Rule." (Diagram 5–18)

When the C is aligned on the outside eye of the split end, he keys through the split end to the quarterback. When the C employs the Sideline Rule, he keys the quarterback and, using his peripheral vision, sees the split end.

When the C reads a pass, he drops into the Deep Outside One-Third Zone and is responsible for that area. He mainly concerns himself with the two receivers to his side. When both the split end and slot execute a vertical release, the C drops between the two and flies to the ball when it is thrown. (Diagram 5–19)

Versus a running play to his side, the C attacks the play from the outside-in and cannot allow himself to be pinned inside by the split end. When the ball is run away from the C, he gains depth first and then flows through the Deep Middle Zone looking for a cutback. (Diagram 5–20)

When the ball is in the middle of the field and both split ends are an equal distance from the ball, the free safety (FS) aligns over the offensive center and is as deep as the wide receivers are split from the ball. When the split ends are split 12 yards from the ball, the FS aligns at a depth of 12 yards. Normally, the FS does not align deeper than 15 yards, no matter how wide the split ends position themselves. (Diagram 5–21) When one split end aligns wider than the other, the FS aligns with his nose on the nose of the offensive guard to the widest receiver side. He aligns as deep as the widest receiver, but never more than 15 yards. (Diagram 5–22)

When the ball is on the hash mark, the FS aligns over the offensive tackle to the wide side of the field. He aligns as deep as the wide split end is split from the ball, but never over 15 yards. (Diagram 5–23)

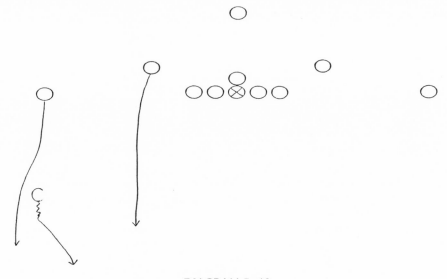

DIAGRAM 5–19

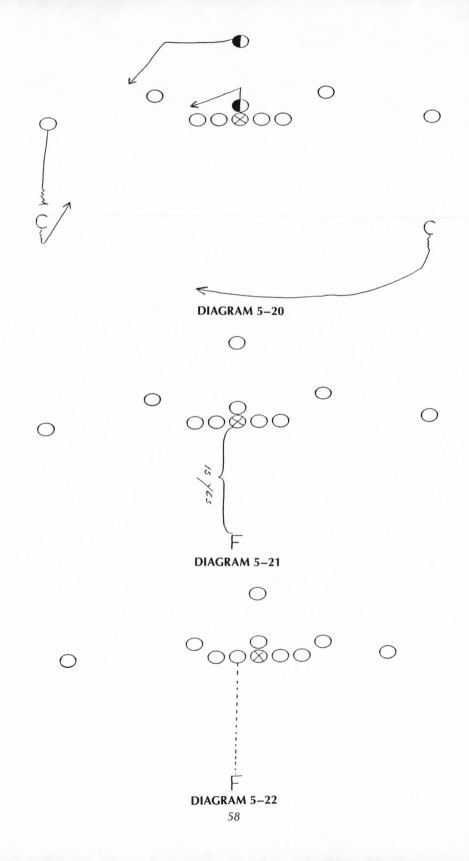

DIAGRAM 5–20

DIAGRAM 5–21

DIAGRAM 5–22

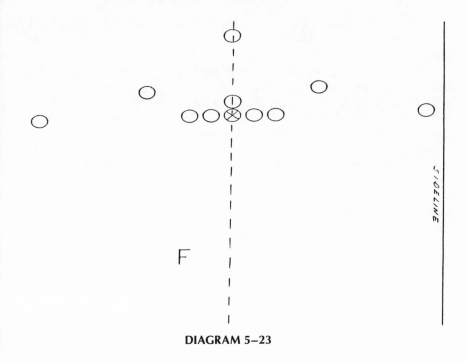

DIAGRAM 5–23

The FS keys the quarterback and, upon recognition of a pass, covers the Deep Middle One-Third Zone.

Versus a run, the FS attacks the play from the inside-out. He is the last line of defense and cannot come up too quickly or out of control.

Versus a Trips Set

Alignment and Assignment

The ILB, away from the Trips set, moves to the middle linebacker (MLB) position. Versus a pass, the MLB keys the running back, and his pass responsibilities depend on the movements of the key.

When the running back moves toward the single-receiver side, the MLB is responsible for the Curl Zone to that side. However, he does not sprint immediately to that area. The MLB knows there is a defender in a Walkaway position to the single-receiver side (the inside OLB or the SS) and only one (the split end) immediate receiving threat aligned to that side. The Walkaway defender covers the split end on any underneath pattern until the Flat Zone is threatened by another receiver. The only other receiver who can quickly attack the Flat Area is the running back. As the MLB sees the running back move toward the single-receiver side, he also moves in that direction.

When the running back blocks, the MLB drops into the Hook Zone and looks for a receiver running a Crossing Pattern from the Trips side of the formation. (Diagram 5–24)

When the running back runs a pattern in the Hook Area, the MLB covers him until he vacates that area. (Diagram 5–25)

When the running back runs into the Flat Area, the MLB sprints directly to the Curl Zone. The MLB knows the job of the Walkaway defender is to cover the Curl Zone until a receiver threatens the Flat Area. (Diagram 5–26)

When the running back goes to the Trips side of the formation, the MLB covers the Hook Zone to that side. However, the MLB realizes there is only one underneath defender to the single-receiver side (OLB or SS) and is very aware of, and picks up, any Crossing Patterns from the Trips side of the formation. (Diagram 5–27)

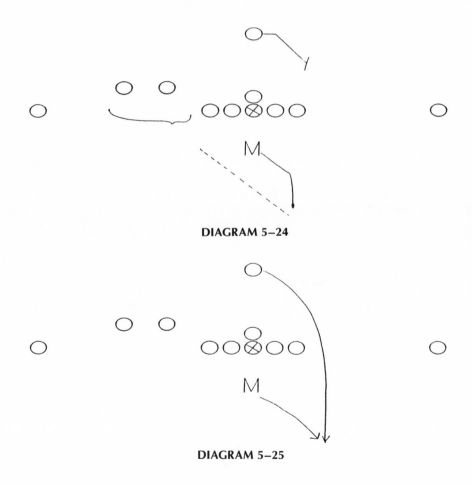

DIAGRAM 5–24

DIAGRAM 5–25

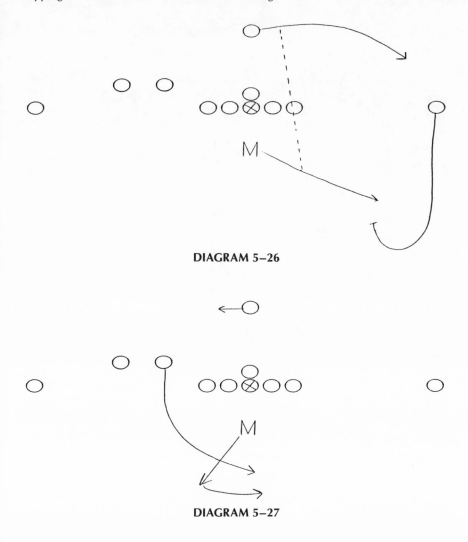

DIAGRAM 5–26

DIAGRAM 5–27

The other ILB, aligned on the inside slot (#3), executes the same techniques employed versus a Double-Slot set. On a Drop-Back Pass, Sprint-Out or Play-Action Pass to his side, the main responsibility of the ILB is the Curl Zone. Versus the Double-Slot set, the ILB goes through the Hook Zone to get to the Curl Area. When a receiver is in the Hook Zone, the ILB covers the receiver until he vacates the zone. Versus the Trips set, his alignment allows him to drop straight back and be in the Hook Zone. Since there are two immediate threats in the Hook Zone (both slots, #2 and #3), the ILB makes sure both receivers are out of the Hook Zone before proceeding to the Curl Area. When both slots execute a vertical release, the ILB drops between them, favoring the inside slot (#3). The drop of the ILB forces

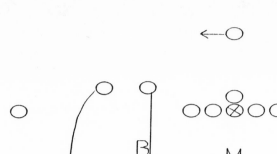

DIAGRAM 5–28

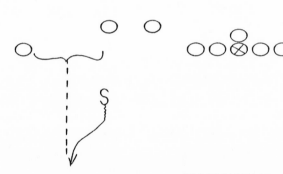

DIAGRAM 5–29

DIAGRAM 5–30

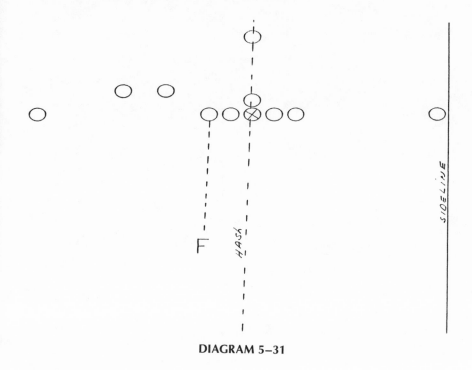

DIAGRAM 5–31

the quarterback to throw over the ILB in order to get the ball to the outside slot (#2). The ILB realizes the MLB, when the running back goes toward the Trips, covers the Hook Zone from the inside-out and helps prevent a Quick Pass to the inside slot (#3). (Diagram 5–28)

The OLB to the side of the call and the SS, when positioned to the side of the Trips, align on the outside slot (#2) at a depth of six yards. From this alignment, the defender executes his basic pass-coverage responsibilities. The OLB or SS drops straight back for a few steps to discourage a Quick Pass to the outside slot (#2). This drop gives the ILB time to drop between the inside and outside slots. From this position, unlike against the Double-Slot set, the OLB or SS does not sprint directly to the Curl Zone. Instead, the defender positions himself between the original alignment of the split end (#1) and the outside slot (#2). The OLB or SS undercovers the Curl Area while being in a position to attack the outside slot (#2) if the ball is thrown to him, and to cover the Flat Area if the ball is thrown there. (Diagram 5–29)

When aligned to the single-receiver side of the Trips set, the OLB or the SS reacts in the same manner as he reacts versus a Double-Slot set when the slot (#2) executes a Crossing Pattern. The Crossing Pattern leaves the defender facing a single split end. However, versus a single split end in a Trips set, the defender initially aligns in a Walkaway position. (Diagram 5–30)

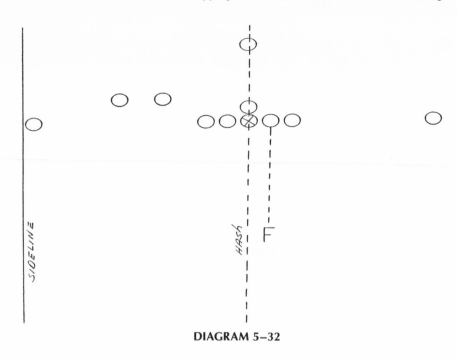

DIAGRAM 5–32

The C aligns and plays in the same manner versus both the Double-Slot and the Trips sets.

Even though the basic pass responsibilities versus the Double-Slot and Trips set are the same for the FS, the alignment changes. When the ball is on the hash mark and the Trips are to the wide side of the field or the ball is in the middle of the field, the FS aligns over the offensive tackle to the side of the Trips. (Diagram 5–31) When the ball is on the hash mark and the Trips are to the sideline side, the FS aligns over the offensive guard to the wide side of the field. The FS pays great attention to the Trips side of the formation but also remains very conscious of the single split end and the possibility of a Post Pattern by that receiver. (Diagram 5-32)

Chapter 6

Employing the Man-Free Secondary with the Over Front

The Man-Free Secondary can be employed with the 3–4 and Over fronts. When the Over front is used, the alignment of the defensive front is the same with the Three-Deep Zone Secondary and the Man-Free Secondary. However, the alignments and assignments of certain defenders change when the Man-Free Secondary is used.

Like the Two-Deep Man-to-Man Secondary (Chapter 3), Man Free is a good coverage to employ in a passing situation. However, it is not as effective in a long-yardage situation as the Two-Deep Man-to-Man coverage. When the Two-Deep Man-to-Man Secondary is employed, there are two defenders covering the deep zones. Man-Free coverage provides only one.

When used without a disguise, Man Free has the same disadvantages as the Two-Deep Man-to-Man Secondary. When the offense puts a slot in motion to create a Trips set, the ILB moves with the slot and shows man-to-man coverage. To help overcome this situation, disguises are often employed, and these are discussed in Chapter 9.

When the offense makes use of the Trips set and when the Two-Deep Man-to-Man Secondary is used, the C to the single-receiver side is put in a difficult situation and, at times, an adjustment must be made to help him with his coverage. This problem is totally eliminated with the Man-Free Secondary. Since an ILB moves out to the side of the Trips, a defender remains in a Walkaway position to the single-split-end side of the formation, and this greatly aids the corner. (Diagrams 6–1 and 6–2)

The Man-Free Secondary, like the Two-Deep Man-to-Man Secondary, has problems defending the Slide Option. These problems are less severe when the offense executes the play from the Double-Slot set. Since there are two inside

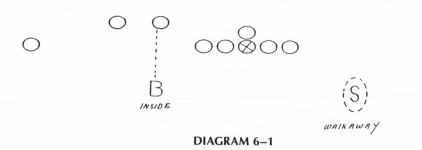

DIAGRAM 6–1

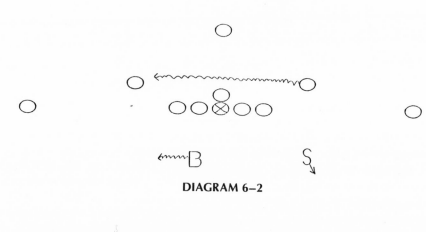

DIAGRAM 6–2

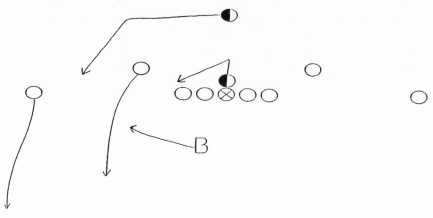

DIAGRAM 6–3

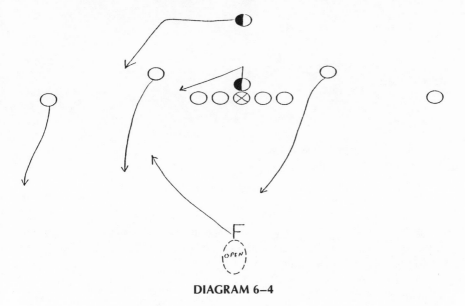

DIAGRAM 6–4

linebackers, it is possible, but difficult, for the playside linebacker to cover the pitch to the running back. (Diagram 6–3)

When the Two-Deep Man-to-Man is used, one of the deep zone defenders can come up and support on the quarterback or running back. The other deep defender can still cover the Deep Middle Zone and play as a free safety. When the Man-Free Secondary is employed, there is only one deep defender. If he comes up to support on the Option, the Deep Middle Zone is left unprotected and is susceptible to a Play-Action Pass. (Diagram 6–4)

ALIGNMENT AND ASSIGNMENT

The ILB employs his normal Over alignment. He is responsible for the third receiver (#3) to his side. In the case of Trips, #3 is the inside slot. When a Double-Slot set is used, #3 is the running back when he releases to the side of the ILB.

When the offense comes out in Trips or motions to Trips, the ILB to the side of the side of the Trips moves out and covers #3. The ILB uses the same techniques and alignments as the OLB, who moves with Trips, in the Two-Deep Man-to-Man Secondary (Chapter 3).

When the slot aligns in Trips, the ILB aligns with his nose on the outside eye of the inside slot (#3). He aligns as far off the line of scrimmage as the slot is split from the offensive tackle, but never more than five yards.

When the offense employs slot motion to create Trips, the ILB runs with the slot and remains one imaginary man in front of him. The ILB remains at a depth of

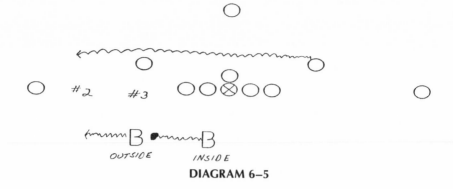

DIAGRAM 6–5

five yards as he mirrors the motion slot. When the motion slot crosses the set slot, the ILB bumps the defender covering the set slot and the ILB covers the original #2 who has become #3. (Diagram 6–5)

Versus Trips or motion to Trips, the ILB plays on the outside eye of the slot and maintains a two-yard cushion. The ILB does not play man-to-man coverage, expecting help from the free safety. He plays as though he is employing pure man-to-man defense.

When the ILB is responsible for the running back (Double-Slot set), he covers the back in much the same way that he covers the slot. He maintains a two-yard cushion and stays on the outside eye of the back. However, he does not cross the line of scrimmage to cover the back in the backfield. The only time he can cross the line of scrimmage is when the ball is thrown to the back in the backfield.

Unlike the OLB, when Two-Deep Man-to-Man is used, the ILB does not make use of a "Squat Technique" versus a slot. This is a difficult technique to master and the ILB would use it so rarely we prefer not to teach it.

Versus a Trips or motion to Trips, the ILB away from the Trips moves to a position in either "A" Gap and maintains his normal depth. In reality, he becomes a middle linebacker (MLB). Since there is a defender in a Walkaway position to the single-split-end side of the formation who is responsible for #2 (running back to his side), the MLB does not have a man to cover unless the running back runs a pattern to the Trips side of the formation. The MLB must then cover the running back as #4. When the running back runs a pattern to the single-split-end side of the formation or does not release, the MLB drops into the Hook Zone to the Trips side of the formation. (Diagram 6–6)

Versus a Double-Slot set, the OLB to the side of the call and the SS align on #2. They align with the nose on the outside eye of the receiver. Their depth is determined by the split of the receiver. They align as deep as #2 is split from the offensive tackle.

The OLB to the side of the call and the SS, when aligned to the side of Trips, align with nose on the outside eye of #2 at a depth of five yards.

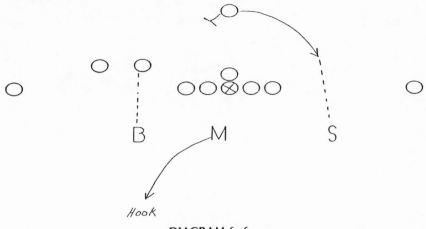

DIAGRAM 6–6

When aligned to the single-split-end side of a Trips set, the SS or OLB employs a Walkaway position. When the running back releases, the defender covers him man to man and uses the same techniques employed by the ILB when he is responsible for the running back. (Diagram 6–7)

The C aligns with his nose on the outside eye of #1 at a depth of six yards. He, like all man-to-man defenders executing the Man-Free Secondary, plays on the outside shoulder of the pass receiver and fights to keep a two-yard cushion. He forces the receiver to the inside toward the free safety. The receiver is actually between the ball and the C. The C is expected to go through the receiver to the ball without committing pass interference. If #1 is fortunate enough to catch the ball, C must strip it out with his free hand. We spend considerable time at practice working on stripping the ball. With practice, this extremely important technique becomes second nature.

There is one exception to the "Outside the Receiver Position." When #1 runs a Fade or any deep outside route, the C moves inside the receiver and squeezes #1 to the sideline. (Diagram 6–8)

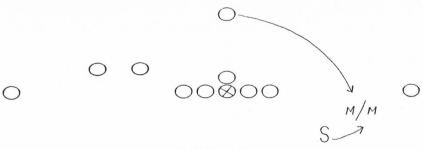

DIAGRAM 6–7

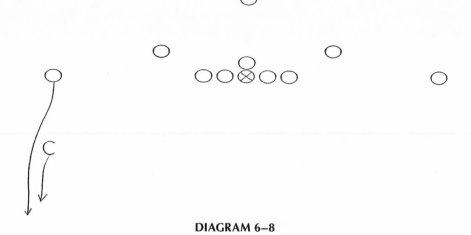

DIAGRAM 6–8

The C cannot get "Stalk-Blocked." He must recognize the block and fight through it to the ball. Once the block is recognized, the C goes through the outside shoulder of the blocker, forcing the blocker to the inside. This forces the ballcarrier toward the free safety. If #1 gets outside position on the C, an outside lane is created and the FS may not get to the ballcarrier. (Diagram 6–9)

The free safety is the key to the successful execution of the Man-Free Secondary. He employs the same alignments used with the Three-Deep Zone Secondary. However, when Man Free is used, he must more accurately read and react to the movements of the quarterback. This is also true for the two safeties when the Two-Deep Man-to-Man Secondary is employed. It is much more important for the free safety in Man Free because there is only one zone defender and he has the full field to cover.

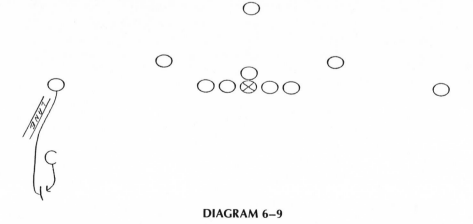

DIAGRAM 6–9

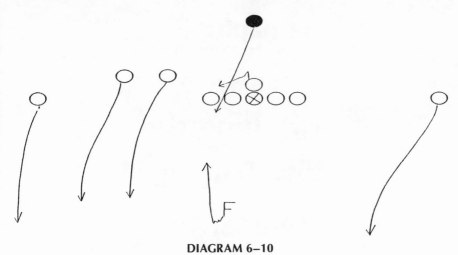

DIAGRAM 6–10

Reading the quarterback is difficult and takes a great deal of practice time. It is well worth the time and effort. It is imperative for the FS to break on the ball before it is thrown. From his original alignment, the FS mirrors the movements of the quarterback and initially reads his numbers. This gives the FS the initial read to determine pass or run. Once a pass is recognized, the FS focuses on the front shoulder of the quarterback and on his front hand. The FS begins to move in the direction the quarterback's front shoulder is pointing while maintaining his original alignment depth. When the front hand of the quarterback leaves the ball, the FS flies in the direction of the quarterback's front shoulder. We have found it to be very rare for a quarterback to release his front hand without continuing and throwing the ball. This technique gives the FS a slight advantage and allows him to come up with more frequent interceptions and pass break-ups.

An FS who waits for the pass to be thrown before breaking on the ball will never give any help on the Fade, Corner, or Skinny Post. The FS who employs our reading techniques will often prevent these patterns from being completed.

The FS is also an integral part of our defense versus the run. He is the only secondary defender who will never be run off by a receiver since he is not executing man-to-man coverage. Therefore, he is the only secondary defender we can count on to quickly read and react to a running play. The FS must be convinced he is both a run and a pass defender. Some free safeties believe their only job is defending the pass. This is very far from the truth. (Diagram 6–10)

The Man-Free Secondary is often employed with a Front Blitz (Chapter 7), and this greatly helps the man-to-man defenders with their coverage.

Chapter 7

Installing the
Blitz Package
Against the
Run and Shoot

THEORY

Those who execute the pure Run and Shoot prefer that the quarterback pass the football on the third step. When the quarterback does release the ball on the third step without any hesitation, a Blitz is a very ineffective defensive tool and a waste of defensive personnel.

The defense, in order to execute an effective Blitz, must do one of two things. The defense can attempt a Blitz only against a team whose quarterback either holds the ball on the third step or executes a pass drop of more than three steps. Although there are some Run-and-Shoot offenses that execute their passing game employing one of these two methods, this is not a very sound defensive foundation upon which to build a Blitz Scheme.

The second alternative, and by far the best, is to prevent the quarterback from throwing on or before the third step. The best way to accomplish this goal is to closely cover all receivers to prevent a quick completion or, at least, to give the quarterback the impression that all receivers are being closely covered by disguising the secondary coverage (Chapter 9).

Never allowing the offense to know when a Blitz is coming is another very important aspect of a successful Blitz Scheme. Although this involves some aspects of disguising (Chapter 9), it is necessary to include it in this chapter to totally comprehend the entire Blitz Package.

There are three important terms involved with the Blitz Scheme. They are Blitz, Show, and Fake. When the word "Blitz" is used, it tells the defense to execute the Blitz from a Basic front (3–4 or Over). The defense aligns in the Basic front and the Blitz is executed on the snap of the ball. Prior to the snap, the offense does not realize a Blitz is about to happen.

When "Show" is called, it tells the defense to align in the actual Blitz position. The inside linebackers align on the line of scrimmage in the gaps they are about to blitz, and the secondary employs Lock alignment. Either the Two-Deep Man-to-Man or the Man-Free Secondary is normally employed. The offense knows a Blitz is about to happen and should do something to defend against it.

When "Fake" is called, it tells the defense to align in a Show position but to execute the non-blitzing defense called in the defensive huddle. This should confuse the offense and force them to do whatever possible to prevent an effective Blitz. The defense executes the non-blitzing call on the snap of the ball. The Show and Fake calls are an absolute necessity to a successful Blitz Scheme.

Like most effective Blitz Packages, our package is based on an overload principle. When a Maximum Blitz is employed, seven defenders are involved in the Blitz and there are four defenders responsible for pass coverage. The offense normally employs six blockers (center, two guards, two tackles, and the running back). One rushing defender should be free. We rarely employ a Maximum Blitz except in a goal-line situation (Chapter 8). We do not particularly want to play with a pure man-to-man coverage in the open field, and a Maximum Blitz forces us to do this.

When a Half Blitz (one side of the ball) is executed, four defenders attack one side of the offensive line. This forces the offensive guard, tackle, and running back to block four defenders. Again, an overload situation exists.

The offense certainly should make use of various blocking schemes to handle an overload situation. It is the job of the defensive coach to devise Blitz Schemes to counter the blocking schemes of the offense and get to the quarterback. This is where scouting reports, film breakdowns, and an excellent defensive coach in the press box pay great dividends on game day.

The Blitz Package includes both "Action" and "Non-Action" Blitzes. An Action Blitz (or Key Blitz) is based upon the movement of a back (Key). The direction of the linebacker Blitz is determined by the movement of the back. When a Non-Action Blitz is employed, the linebacker Blitz is predetermined. It is not dependent upon the action of any offensive player, and the Blitz occurs on the snap of the ball. Even though we use Non-Action Blitzes versus the Run and Shoot, we prefer employing Action Blitzes. They are more effective against this offense. Since the Maximum Blitz is covered in Chapter 8, only the Half Blitz is covered in this chapter.

HALF BLITZ

There is an unlimited number of Half Blitz possibilities. In our Basic Defensive Package, we include many different Half Blitzes. We also develop additional Blitzes as part of a particular game plan and have created a Blitz or two during a game. This chapter includes several Blitzes, often employed versus the Run-and-Shoot offense, that are part of our Basic Defensive Package. The Half Blitz is called according to the offensive strength. The Blitz is called to either the strong side or the weak side of the offensive formation. The following are our basic strength rules:

1. When the offense employs Trips or motions to Trips, strength is to the side of Trips.

2. When the offense employs a Double-Slot set and the ball is on the hash, strength is to the wide side of the field.

3. When the offense employs a Double-Slot set and the ball is in the middle of the field, strength is to the defensive left.

This chapter includes the following Half Blitzes:

1. 3–4 Action Blitz

2. 3–4 Non-Action Blitz

3. Over Action Blitz

4. Over Non-Action Blitz

The 3–4 Action Blitz Strong vs. a Double-Slot Set

The 3–4 Action Blitz is normally executed with the Man-Free Secondary. Prior to the snap of the ball, the defensive front aligns in a Basic 3–4 alignment. However, the secondary aligns in a Two-Deep Man-to-Man Lock alignment to disguise the Man-Free Secondary and to prevent a Quick Pass.

The N attacks the weakside shoulder of the offensive center and is responsible for the weakside "A" Gap. The ends slant to the outside shoulder of the offensive guards and are responsible for the "B" Gaps.

The play of the four linebackers is the key to the effectiveness of the Blitz. The OLB's employ Lock alignment and key the setback. On the snap of the ball, they collide with the slot and react to the movement of the setback. When the setback goes away from the OLB, he plays the slot man to man and executes his normal man-to-man coverage techniques. When the setback steps toward the OLB, the OLB executes a Blitz through the outside shoulder of the slot and is responsible for the "D" Gap.

The ILB's also key the setback. When the setback steps to the strong side, the strongside ILB blitzes the strongside "C" Gap and is responsible for that gap. The weakside ILB blitzes the strongside "A" Gap and is responsible for that gap. When the setback steps to the weak side, the weakside ILB blitzes the weakside "C" Gap and is responsible for that gap. The strongside ILB flows to the weak side and is free to go to the ball.

The ILB who blitzes the "C" Gap is given "Blitz Peel" responsibility. When the setback (#3) releases for a pass, the ILB breaks off the Blitz and picks up the setback using man-to-man coverage. This eliminates #3 as a pass threat, and the quarterback is still contained by the blitzing OLB.

The C's play #1 with Man-to-Man Lock, and the S's read the movement of the setback. When the setback steps to the strong side, the FS rotates up and covers the slot man to man. The SS rotates to the Deep Middle Zone and plays as an FS. When the setback steps to the weak side, the SS rotates up and covers the slot man to man while the FS rotates into the Deep Middle Zone and is free. (Diagrams 7–1 and 7–2)

This Blitz has one serious weakness. When the offense executes a Bootleg Pass or Run, there is no defender to contain the quarterback. The OLB and ILB, to the side of the Bootleg (away from the action of the setback), are removed from the possibility of containing the quarterback. The ILB blitzes the "A" Gap to the side of the setback and the OLB covers the slot man to man. This problem can be eliminated by keying the quarterback rather than the setback. However, this can be a slower key and can cause problems. (Diagram 7–3)

The 3–4 Non-Action Blitz Weak vs. a Trips Set

The 3–4 Non-Action Blitz is normally employed with the Man-Free Secondary, with the Two-Deep Man-to-Man Lock alignment used as a disguise.

The N attacks the strongside shoulder of the offensive center and is

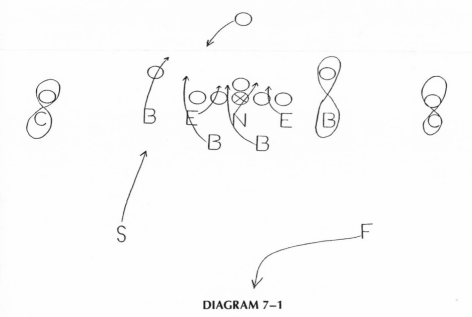

DIAGRAM 7–1

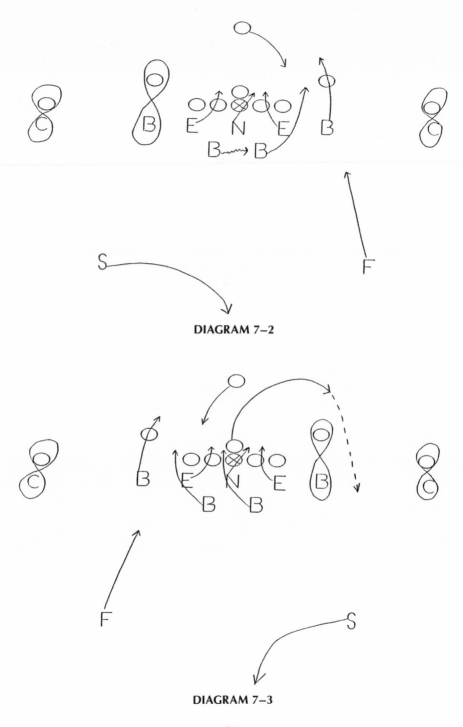

DIAGRAM 7–2

DIAGRAM 7–3

responsible for the strongside "A" Gap. The ends charge through the outside shoulder of the offensive tackles and are responsible for the "C" Gaps.

The ILB's key the movement of the ball and not an offensive player. The weakside ILB blitzes the weakside "D" Gap and is responsible for that gap. He also has Blitz Peel responsibility when the setback runs a pattern to his side. The strongside ILB blitzes the weakside "A" Gap and is responsible for that gap and does not have Blitz Peel responsibility.

The OLB, to the side of the Trips set, moves out on the outside slot (#2). The OLB, from the other side of the formation, moves over to cover the inside slot (#3). Both employ Lock and prevent any Quick Pass to either slot.

The C's employ Man-to-Man Lock versus the split ends (#1), and the S's are ready to rotate on the snap of the ball. The FS begins to slowly "Cheat Up" prior to the snap. He does not want to alert the quarterback to a possible Safety Blitz. On the snap of the ball, the FS blitzes the "B" Gap and is responsible for that gap. The SS rotates to the Deep Middle Zone and plays as an FS. (Diagram 7–4)

This Blitz also has two weaknesses. If the setback runs the ball in the strongside "B" Gap, the only defender who can make the play is the SS. If he makes the play, it will be after a significant gain. (Diagram 7–5)

The other weakness involves any pass to the setback to the Trips side of the formation. There is no defender left to cover the setback (#4) if he runs a pass

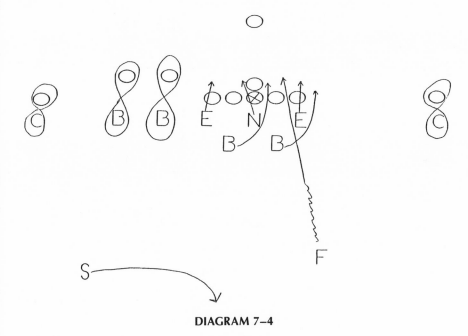

DIAGRAM 7–4

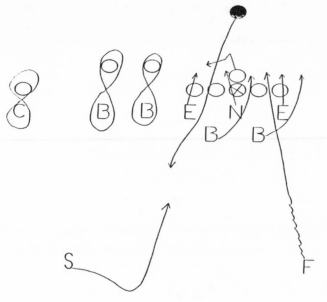

DIAGRAM 7–5

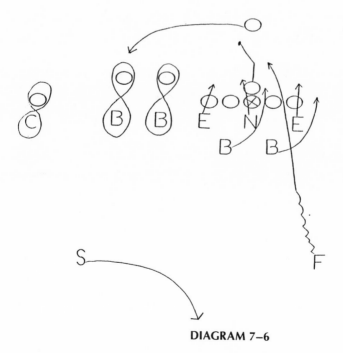

DIAGRAM 7–6

pattern to the strong side. However, if the setback does run a pattern to the Trips side, he cannot block to the weak side and, hopefully, one of the weakside blitzers will get to the quarterback before he can release the ball. (Diagram 7–6)

The Over Weak Action Blitz vs. a Double-Slot Set

The Over Action Blitz is normally executed with a Man-Free Lock Secondary. The front aligns in an Over Weak and the secondary aligns in a Man-Free Lock alignment.

The N, both E's, and the strongside OLB employ their normal Over alignment and attack the offensive players on whom they are aligned and assume their normal gap responsibilities.

The ILB's assume their normal Over alignment and key the setback. When the setback steps to the strong side, the strongside ILB blitzes the strongside "D" Gap and is responsible for that gap and has Blitz Peel responsibility. The weakside ILB blitzes the strongside "A" Gap and is responsible for that gap. When the setback steps to the weak side, the weakside ILB blitzes the weakside "D" Gap and is responsible for that gap and has Blitz Peel responsibility. The strongside ILB blitzes the weakside "B" Gap and is responsible for that gap.

The C's employ Man-to-Man Lock coverage versus the split ends (#1). The SS and weakside OLB employ their normal Man-Free alignment and use man-to-man coverage against the slots (#2). The FS executes his basic Man-Free responsibilities. (Diagram 7–7)

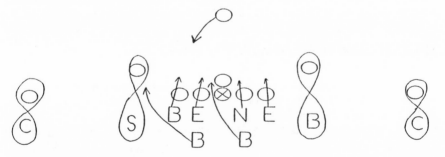

F

DIAGRAM 7–7

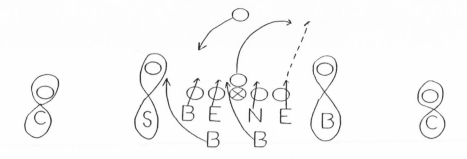

F

DIAGRAM 7–8

Unlike the 3–4 Action Blitz, the Over Action Blitz is much more effective against a quarterback Bootleg Pass or Run. Since the E (to the side of the front call) and the OLB (away from the side of the front call) do not key the setback and are responsible for the "C" Gaps, the quarterback is contained and prevented from turning the corner. (Diagram 7–8)

The Over Weak Non-Action Blitz vs. a Trips Set

The Over Non-Action Blitz is normally employed with the Man-Free Lock Secondary. The ILB, to the side of the Trips, moves out to cover the inside slot (#3). This makes the remaining ILB a middle linebacker.

The N, weakside E, and strongside OLB employ their normal Over alignment and attack the offensive players on whom they are aligned and assume their normal Gap responsibilities. However, the strongside E does not execute his basic Over techniques. The strongside E employs his normal alignment but slants to the strongside shoulder of the offensive center. This move should eliminate the center as a weakside protector and help make the Blitz more successful.

The strongside ILB moves out to cover the inside slot (#3) but does not employ a Lock technique. The ILB aligns as deep as the slot is split from the offensive tackle and plays man-to-man coverage from that alignment. The MLB aligns in the weakside "A" Gap at his normal depth. On the snap of the ball, he blitzes the weakside "B" Gap and is responsible for that gap.

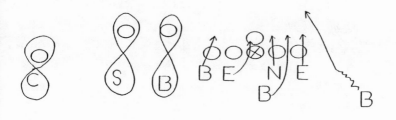

F

DIAGRAM 7–9

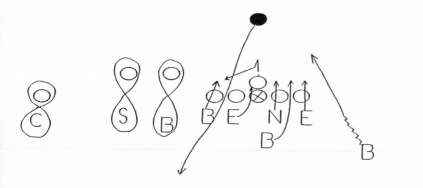

F

DIAGRAM 7–10

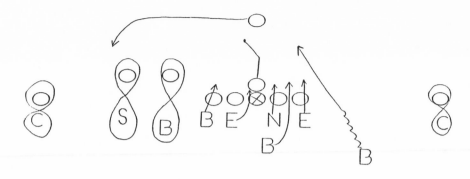

F

DIAGRAM 7–11

The weakside OLB aligns in a Walkaway position. Prior to the snap of the ball, the OLB begins to "Cheat Up." On the snap of the ball, he blitzes the "D" Gap. He maintains "D" Gap responsibility and also has Blitz Peel if the setback executes a pass pattern to his side.

The C's and the SS employ Man-to-Man Lock coverage versus their receivers, and the FS executes his Man-Free responsibilities. (Diagram 7–9)

This Blitz has the same two weaknesses as the 3–4 Non-Action Blitz. The strongside "B" Gap is vulnerable to a run by the setback, and the offense may find success by throwing a pass to the setback running a pattern to the Trips side (strong side). However, the quarterback should be sacked by a blitzer before throwing any pass to the strong side. (Diagrams 7–10 and 7–11)

Chapter 8

Defensing the Run and Shoot with the Goal-Line Package

THEORY

The Run and Shoot presents some unique problems in a goal-line situation. Most defensive teams execute some form of a goal-line defense that differs from the defensive schemes employed between the 10-yard lines. These specialized goal-line defenses are not very effective versus the Run-and-Shoot offense. We use the same defenses on the goal line, with minor modifications, as those employed between the 10-yard lines. The modifications primarily involve secondary coverages and have little effect on the defensive front.

THE GOAL-LINE FRONT

The 3–4 and the Over fronts are employed in the goal-line situations. However, Action and Non-Action Blitzes are often used and these include both Maximum and Half Blitzes. Both Show and Fake are employed most of the time and are responsible for much of our goal-line success. Blitz Peel is in effect to prevent the setback from slipping out and catching a pass or being a successful receiver of a pitch on the Slide Option.

THE GOAL-LINE SECONDARY

Since the front is so aggressive and a Blitz is employed most of the time, pure man-to-man pass coverage is used in the goal-line situation. Pure man to man is employed, but the most common form of man coverage executed on the goal line is Man Match. This coverage is explained later in this chapter.

Unlike many defensive teams, particularly versus the Run-and-Shoot offense, we employ a type of zone coverage in goal-line situations. This coverage is known as Fox and is used with both fronts, particularly when a Blitz is employed. The use of Show and Fake helps make this coverage even more effective since most offensive teams expect man-to-man coverage to accompany a Blitz.

Whenever we are involved in a goal-line situation, the secondary and any LB covering a slot make use of two different alignments. They are "Lock" and "Normal." When Normal is employed, the defender aligns five yards off the receiver but never in the End Zone. Using these two alignments prevents the offense from determining a man-to-man or zone coverage prior to the snap of the ball and helps make the Fox coverage even more effective.

Man-to-Man Secondary

The secondary defenders and any LB covering a slot align with their nose on the inside or outside eye of the receiver. Aligning on the inside or outside eye of the receiver is determined by the scouting reports. At times, the defender will initially align on one eye and move to the other prior to the snap of the ball.

When the 3–4 front and the basic Man-to-Man Secondary are employed, the C's cover the split ends (#1) and the SS covers the slot (#2) to the strong side. The FS covers the slot (#2) to the weak side versus a Double-Slot formation and the inside slot (#3) versus a Trips set. When motion is used to create Trips, the safety runs across the formation with the motion slot and "Bumps" the other safety when the motion slot crosses the set slot. (Diagrams 8–1 and 8–2)

When the Over front and the basic Man-to-Man Secondary are employed versus a Double-Slot set, the C's cover the split ends (#1). The SS and OLB (to the side of the front call) cover the slots (#2) and the FS is free. (Diagram 8–3)

Versus the Trips set, the FS comes up and covers the inside slot. This is not the way the Trips set is covered between the 10-yard lines. Normally, one of the ILB's moves out on the inside slot. In a goal-line situation, there is no need to have a free safety, unlike in the open field. It is also much more beneficial to have two ILB's for Blitz purposes on the goal line. When the Trips set is away from the OLB (to the side of the call) or the SS, this defender is responsible for #2; #2 is normally the setback running a pattern to the weak side. (Diagram 8–4)

When the Man-to-Man Secondary is used, the defenders covering receivers are expected to stay with their men throughout the entire play. There is no switching

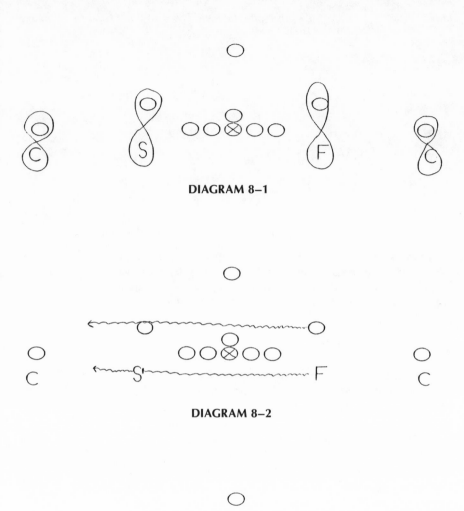

DIAGRAM 8–1

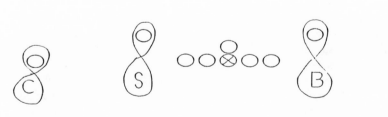

DIAGRAM 8–2

F
DIAGRAM 8–3

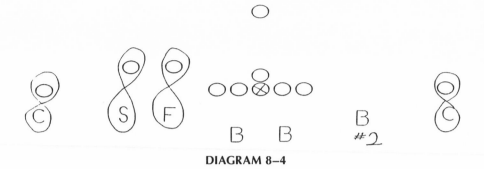

DIAGRAM 8–4

of receivers on Crossing Patterns. To help eliminate the possibility of being "Picked Off," especially versus a Trips set, the defenders vary their alignment depth, and this helps solve the problem. A real remedy to the pick-off problem is either the Man-Match Secondary or the Fox Secondary.

Man-Match Secondary

Many Run-and-Shoot offenses employ "Picks" to get receivers free when they face a Man-to-Man Secondary. This is particularly true in a goal-line situation. The Man-to-Man Secondary is susceptible to this type of attack. One way to neutralize the "Pick play" is to employ the Man-Match Secondary.

The alignment rules for the pass defenders are the same for the Man-Match and the Man-to-Man Secondaries. However, when the Man-Match Secondary is employed, the pass defenders align at Normal depth and do not use Lock. The rule for the pass defender is to cover his man or whoever becomes his man. In other words, the defender who is responsible for #1, prior to the snap of the ball, is responsible for whoever becomes #1 after the ball is snapped. When the split end (#1) releases inside and the outside slot (Trips set) goes outside, the C picks up the outside slot because the outside slot becomes #1, or the widest receiver. The defender originally responsible for the outside slot (#2), picks up the split end who has become #2, or the second widest receiver. (Diagram 8–5)

When the Man-Match Secondary is employed, the ILB's are never involved in a Blitz. The ILB is normally responsible for the setback (#2, #3, or #4, depending on the formation and front call). However, the ILB must cover the slot when the slot comes inside and the setback goes outside. (Diagram 8–6)

The Man-Match Secondary works very well against the Pick play. A typical Run-and-Shoot Pick play in a goal-line situation is run from the Trips set. The three receivers (Trips) release inside and hope the man-to-man defenders follow them inside. The inside slot attempts to "Pick" the ILB and free up the setback running a

DIAGRAM 8–5

Flair Pattern to the strong side. The outside slot attempts to "Pick" the defender covering the inside slot, and the split end attempts to "Pick" the defender covering the outside slot. The defender covering the split end is expected to go inside with the split end, leaving no defender to cover the pattern by the setback.

When the Man-Match Secondary is employed, the defenders cover the correct receivers after the snap of the ball. The ILB covers the inside slot who becomes #4. The defender initially responsible for the inside slot (#3 prior to the snap of the ball) covers the outside slot who becomes #3. The defender initially responsible for the outside slot (#2 prior to the snap of the ball) covers the split end who becomes #2, and the defender initially responsible for the split end (#1) covers the setback who becomes #1. (Diagram 8–7)

On paper, this seems like a very simple exchange of responsibilities. It is not! This coverage takes a great deal of communication between the defenders and hours of practice, but it is well worth the effort. Perhaps a simpler means of protecting against the Pick play and one that takes much less practice time is the Fox Secondary.

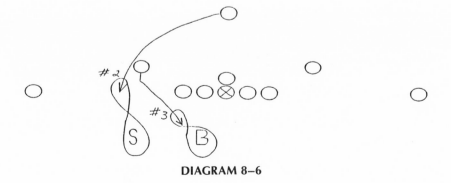

DIAGRAM 8–6

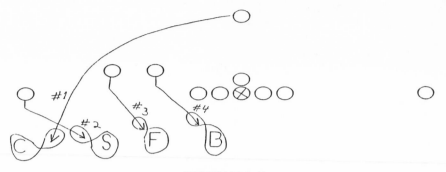

DIAGRAM 8–7

Fox Secondary

The Fox Secondary is a zone coverage, like the Man-to-Man Secondary and the Man-Match Secondary, employed only in goal-line situations. Since this coverage requires no involvement by the ILB's, the front normally executes a Blitz when the Fox Secondary is used. The pass defenders employ the same alignments used with the Man-Match Secondary.

When employed with a 3–4 front, the Fox Secondary is a four-deep zone coverage. Each secondary defender is expected to cover one-fourth of the field. This coverage is excellent versus a Double-Slot set, but certain problems exist versus the Trips set.

Versus a Double-Slot set, the C's cover the Outside One-Fourth Zones, and the S's cover the Inside One-Fourth Zones. (Diagram 8–8)

Versus the Trips set, the FS, employing the Man-Match Secondary alignment, aligns on the inside slot. From this position, he has a very difficult time getting to his Inside One-Fourth Zone on the snap of the ball. This leaves the area vulnerable

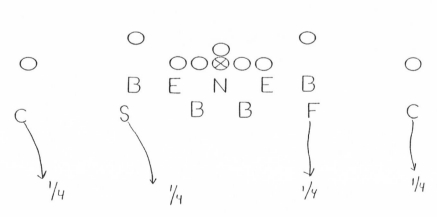

DIAGRAM 8–8

to a Post Pattern by the weakside split end. (Diagram 8–9) Although effective versus the Pick play, the Fox Secondary does have problems to the weak side versus a Trips set. For this reason, we prefer to use the Fox Secondary with the Over front, particularly in a passing situation.

The Fox Secondary with the Over front provides five zone pass defenders while the Fox Secondary with the 3–4 front provides only four. This gives each pass defender a smaller area of responsibility. Versus a Double-Slot set, the C's cover the Outside One-Fifth Zones. The SS and the OLB (to the side of the front call) cover the next One-Fifth Zones while the FS covers the Middle One-Fifth Zone.

Versus the Trips set, the FS moves to align on the inside slot. However, unlike the Fox Secondary with the 3–4 front, there is a defender in a Walkaway position to the weak side. This defender helps prevent a successful Post Pattern to the split end and allows the FS to favor the strong side (Trips side) of the formation. (Diagram 8–10)

The Fox Secondary with the Over front is excellent versus the Pick play. Not expecting zone coverage, the three receivers (Trips) release inside, but the defenders do not go with them and the offensive play is not successful.

Looking at two of our most commonly used goal-line defenses, shows the combination of the Blitz front and the goal-line secondary.

3–4 OLB GO—MAN-MATCH SECONDARY

All front defenders assume their normal 3–4 alignment. The N attacks the offensive center and is responsible for both "A" Gaps. The N is responsible for the Draw play and does not execute a hard pass rush. The E's are responsible for the "C" Gaps and for putting on a hard pass rush.

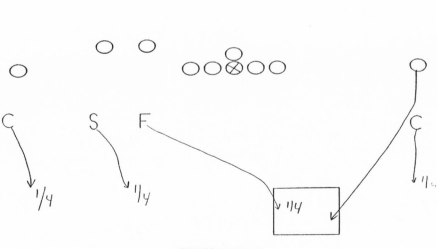

DIAGRAM 8–9

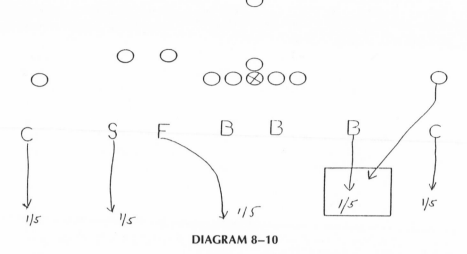

DIAGRAM 8-10

The OLB's execute a Blitz and are responsible for outside contain. They prevent the quarterback from getting to the perimeter. The ILB's are responsible for the "B" Gaps. The strongside ILB is responsible for #4 on a pass, and the weakside ILB is responsible for #2 on a pass. When the setback goes to the strong side, the weakside ILB is free and should help the weakside C with any inside Pass Pattern run by the split end. The secondary executes the Man-Match Secondary.

This defensive combination is excellent in a long-yardage goal-line situation (second down and greater than eight yards, or third down and greater than five yards). (Diagram 8-11)

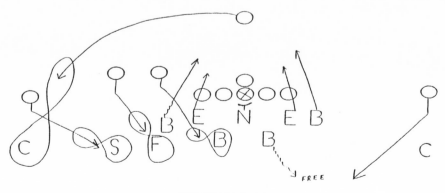

DIAGRAM 8-11

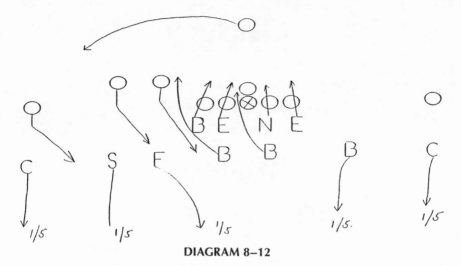

DIAGRAM 8–12

OVER WEAK ACTION BLITZ—FOX SECONDARY

The front four defenders (the weakside N and E and the strongside E and OLB) assume their normal Over alignment and have their normal gap responsibilities. They are expected to put on a hard pass rush.

Versus Trips, in a goal-line situation, no ILB moves out on the inside slot. This leaves two ILB's to execute an effective Blitz. When the ILB Key (setback) steps to the strong side, the strongside ILB blitzes the "D" Gap and must contain the quarterback. The strongside ILB does not have Blitz Peel responsibility because the secondary is employing a zone coverage. With no Blitz Peel responsibility, the strongside ILB can rush with reckless abandon. The weakside ILB blitzes the strongside "A" Gap and looks for any Draw play before going to the quarterback. The secondary executes the Fox Secondary.

This defensive combination is used in any goal-line situation. It is equally effective against a running play or a passing play. (Diagram 8–12)

Chapter 9

Disguising
the Defenses

Modern offenses employ pre-snap shifts, motions, and many other legal maneuvers to help deceive the defense. These tactics, and many others, should be used by the defense to confuse offensive pre-snap and post-snap reads, blocking schemes, and pass patterns. It is time for the defensive coaches to become much more offensive.

We practice various disguises against all offenses. However, versus the Run and Shoot, defensive trickery is an essential ingredient to success. The Run and Shoot depends so heavily on pre- and post-snap reads by the quarterback and the receivers that a non-disguised defense is destined for failure.

There is an unlimited number of possible disguises to any defensive scheme. We have basic disguises we practice from the first day of pre-season football camp and disguises we develop for individual opponents. This chapter deals with our basic disguise package. When a disguise is employed, the disguise is called in the defensive huddle prior to the actual defense. The following is a sample call:

From 3–4 Look, Jump Over Weak—Shift Three-Deep Zone

3–4 LOOK

When the 3–4 Look is used as a disguise, the front aligns in a Basic 3–4. To move to an Over from this alignment, the five defenders (two OLB's, two E's, and an N) can either Jump or Slant. When Jump is used, the defenders move to the called front prior to the snap of the ball. In the sample call, the front is aligned in a 3–4, and on a call from one of the ILB's, they jump to an Over Weak alignment. (Diagram 9–1)

O

O   O

O   OO⊗OO   O

  B   ↗E→ N→ E→
            B   B   B↘

DIAGRAM 9–1

When Slant is selected as the means to go from one front to another, the defenders execute a Slant on the snap of the ball and move from a 3–4 alignment to an Over Weak alignment. The weakside (onside) OLB does not use a Slant technique to get to his new alignment. He simply moves on the snap of the ball to his new position. (Diagram 9–2)

When the 3–4 Look is used as a disguise, the secondary employs a Two-Deep Secondary alignment. The secondary defenders can move from one secondary to another by employing either Shift or Slide. When Shift is used, the secondary defenders move to the called secondary prior to the snap of the ball. In the sample call, the secondary defenders move to a Three-Deep Zone Secondary on a call from the FS. This forces the quarterback and receivers to make a very quick pre-snap read. (Diagram 9–3)

When Slide is employed, the secondary defenders move to the called secondary on the snap of the ball. This totally eliminates any pre-snap read by the offensive players.

When the 3–4 Look and the Blitz Look are employed, both the front and the secondary execute a disguise. However, there are many instances when only the front or the secondary executes a disguise. These are covered later in this chapter.

DIAGRAM 9–2

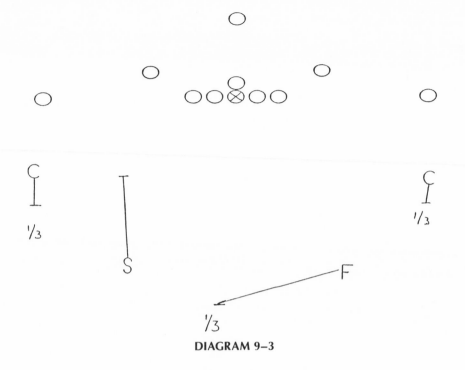

DIAGRAM 9–3

BLITZ LOOK

The Blitz Look disguise is used much more frequently versus the Run and Shoot than is the 3–4 Look. We want to keep the Run-and-Shoot quarterback concerned about our Blitz Package. This gives him, and the rest of the offense, one more thing about which to worry and makes us much more effective when we do execute the Blitz.

When the Blitz Look is used as a disguise, the front aligns in a Fake 3–4 Non-Action Blitz Strong (Chapter 7), and the secondary employs a Man-Free Lock alignment. When the front is going to move to an Over alignment, Jump or Slant is to be employed. When the secondary is going to change alignment, Shift or Slide is again used. (Remember, the front can employ Fake without involving the secondary; see Chapter 7.) However, when the front uses Fake without the secondary employing Man-Free Lock, it is not considered a Blitz Look disguise, just a Fake disguise. The following is a sample call:

From Blitz Look, Jump 3–4—Shift Two-Deep Zone

The N, E's, and OLB's do not have to move since they are already aligned in a 3–4 front. The ILB's, prior to the snap of the ball, move from the Fake alignment to their normal 3–4 alignment. The secondary, on the command of the FS, moves from the Man-Free Lock alignment to the Two-Deep Zone alignment. (Diagram 9–4)

When Jump or Shift is used, it is extremely important to know the various starting counts (cadence) of the opponent. This information must be part of the scouting report. Anticipating the starting count allows the defenders to shift just prior to the snap of the ball. This move confuses any pre-snap reads by the offensive team and forces most of the offensive players to make mental adjustments very quickly. The Jump adversely affects offensive blocking schemes, and the Shift confuses quarterback and receiver reads.

If the ball is snapped prior to the Jump or Shift, the defensive players move on the snap of the ball. This changes the Jump and Shift to the Slant and Slide. Both pre-snap and post-snap moves are effective, and both should be employed during the game. Using only one or the other takes a valuable deceptive tactic away from the defensive game plan.

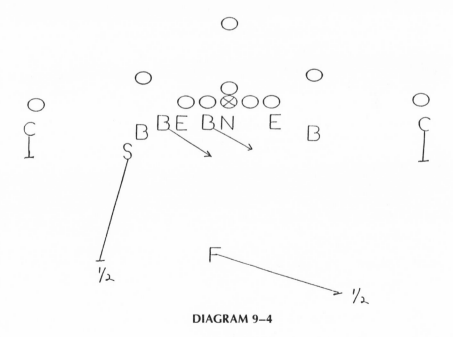

DIAGRAM 9–4

INDIVIDUAL SECONDARY AND FRONT DISGUISES

There are many instances when either a front or a secondary disguise is employed during a game. Versus the Run and Shoot, we disguise our secondary 90 percent of the time. Delaying or confusing the pre- and post-snap reads of the quarterback and receivers is vital to stopping this potent offense.

When the 3–4 front is employed, the secondary initially employs a Two-Deep Zone alignment or a Man-Free Lock alignment. From either of these initial alignments, the secondary uses Shift or Slide to move to the called secondary.

When the 3–4 front is employed and the secondary uses the Two-Deep Zone alignment, the following secondaries can be executed from this alignment or moved to by using either Shift or Slide:

1. Two-Deep Zone

2. Two-Deep Read

3. Two-Deep Man to Man

4. Three-Deep Zone

5. Man Free

The following is a sample call:

3–4—From Two-Deep Zone, Shift Three-Deep Zone

The front executes the 3–4 front. The secondary uses the Two-Deep Zone alignment and, on the call of the FS, Shifts to the Three-Deep Zone Secondary. (Diagram 9–5)

When the 3–4 front is used and the secondary employs the Man-Free Lock alignment, the following secondaries can be executed from this alignment or moved to by using either Shift or Slide:

1. Two-Deep Zone

2. Two-Deep Read

3. Two-Deep Man to Man

4. Three-Deep Zone

5. Man Free (Man-Free Lock)

6. Man to Man (Goal Line)

The following is a sample call:

3–4—From Man-Free Lock, Slide Two-Deep Zone

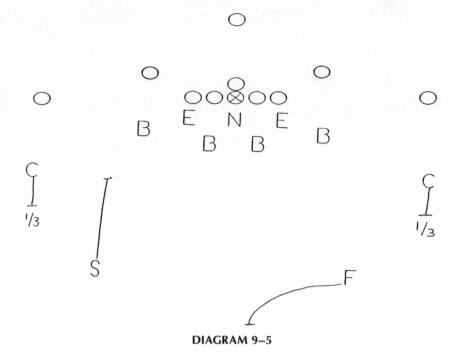

DIAGRAM 9–5

The front executes the 3–4 front. The secondary uses the Man-Free Lock alignment and, on the snap of the ball, Slides to the Two-Deep Zone Secondary. (Diagram 9–6)

Versus the Run-and-Shoot offense, a Three-Deep Secondary is normally employed with the Over front. This limits the number of secondary disguises used. When the Over front is used, the secondary initially employs a Three-Deep Zone alignment (SS to the strong side) or a Man-Free Lock alignment.

When the Over front is used and the secondary employs the Three-Deep Zone alignment, the following secondaries can be executed from this alignment or moved to by using either Shift or Slide:

1. Three-Deep Zone

2. Three-Deep Zone Weak

3. Man Free

The following is a sample call:

Over Weak—From Three-Deep Zone, Man Free

The front executes the Over front. The secondary, from the Three-Deep Zone alignment, executes the Man-Free Secondary. (Diagram 9–7)

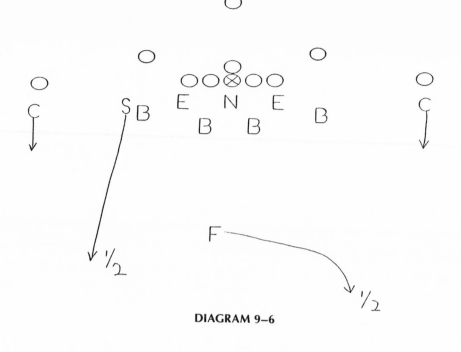

DIAGRAM 9–6

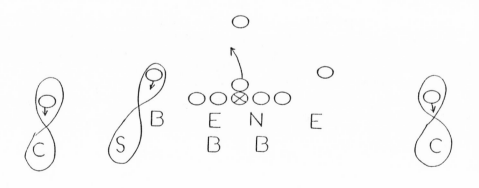

DIAGRAM 9–7

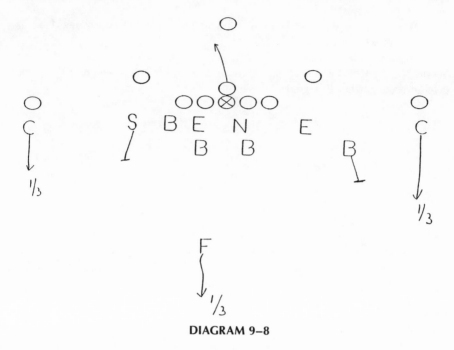

DIAGRAM 9–8

When the Over front is used and the secondary employs the Man-Free Lock alignment, the following secondaries can be executed from this alignment or moved to by using either Shift or Slide:

1. Three-Deep Zone

2. Three-Deep Zone Weak

3. Man-Free Lock (Man Free)

4. Man to Man (Goal Line)

The following is a sample call:

Over Weak—From Man-Free Lock, Slide Three-Deep Zone

The front executes the Over front. The secondary, on the snap of the ball, Slides from the Man-Free Lock to the Three-Deep Zone Weak Secondary. (Diagram 9–8)

The front also executes disguises without involving the secondary. However, these are employed far less than the secondary disguises. We prefer to use the combination disguises (3–4 Look and the Blitz Look) to disguise the front.

When a front disguise is used, without involving the secondary, Fake is normally employed (Chapter 7).

Disguise is a real key to defensive success, particularly versus the Run and Shoot. It is imperative to keep the offensive team off-balance, and disguising the defense accomplishes this goal.

HARDING PRESS
P.O. BOX 141
HAWORTH, NJ 07641
(201) 767-7114

No. of Copies

HP001   DEFENSING THE DELAWARE WING-T

B. Kenig $12.00   _____

This guide offers the innovative use of the 3–4 "Slant" and
"Read Blitz," which present major problems for the dynamic
Wing-T.

HP002   FOOTBALL'S EXPLOSIVE MULTI-BONE ATTACK

T. DeMeo $12.00   _____

The Multi-Bone combines the Veer's explosiveness, the I's
power, the Wing-T's misdirection, the Wishbone's ball control,
and the wide-open play of the Pro Dropback Passing game.

HP003   COACHING RUN-AND-SHOOT FOOTBALL

A. Black $12.00   _____

This guide gives you all the pass routes, plus blocking schemes,
a complementary offense, a one-back running game, and much
more.

HP004   COACHING THE DEFENSIVE BACKFIELD

G. McMackin $12.00   _____

The defensive backfield coach at the University of Miami
provides a guide to all facets of defensive secondary play with
exacting fundamentals, game-like drills, and game-day
strategies.

HP005   THE EAGLE FIVE-LINEBACKER DEFENSE

Fritz Shurmur $12.00   _____

The Phoenix Cardinals' defensive coordinator presents a unique
and innovative scheme that's applicable to any defensive plan.

Please send check, M.O., or school P.O. with your order.

Name _____   Subtotal: _____

Address _____   (NJ Residents Only—

_____   6% Sales Tax) _____

City _____   *Shipping   _____

State _____ Zip _____   Total: _____

Phone (   ) _____

*Shipping: $2.00 first book plus 75¢ for each additional book